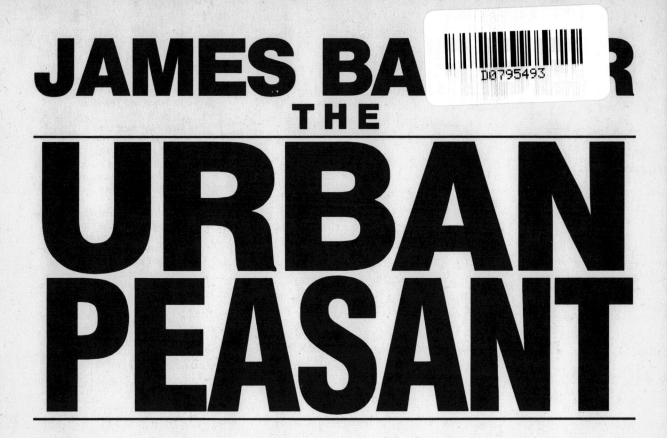

JAMES BARBER

THE

URBAN
PEASANT

MORE THAN A COOKBOOK

Dedicated to
Jonathun and Theodore

First Published 1989
Second Printing 1990
Third Printing 1992
by Urban Peasant Productions Ltd.
P.O. Box 5157, Vancouver, B.C.
© by James Barber

3rd ed.
ISBN 0-9694144-0-4

Illustrations by Kristin Krimmel
Cover designed by
Westbound Publishing House Ltd.
Printed and bound in Canada.

INTRODUCTION

There's a shortage of grandmothers in most kitchens — good old fashioned grandmothers who could chop an onion with one hand, and knit a winter muffler with the other. Meanwhile, they talked, burped the baby, listened, patted the dog, took a pinch of this and a bit of that, and thirty minutes later, with no effort at all, had supper on the table.

Good food doesn't have to be complicated, or expensive. Most of all, it doesn't have to be perfect — food is to eat, not to be photographed. Just as a lot of perfectly good weddings are ruined for the sake of an album, so too many good dinners are spoiled by worry.

This book is not a gourmet manual — it's a book mostly of pleasure, a collection of things I've eaten, cooked and enjoyed in half the countries of the world. Most of it is simple, peasant food, using ingredients which are available at most supermarkets. It's a book of grandma food, complete with all the long rambling stories that go so well with comfortable, relaxed cooking.

It's easier than you think.

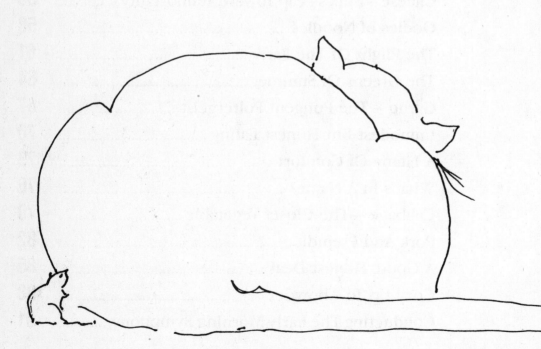

CONTENTS

New Year's Procrastinations

Don't rush into anything drastic. Simmer up a nice pot of soup, put your feet up and make a list.

Smoking, drinking and over-eating — by mid-January we're mostly all back on the wagon of self-indulgence that we so desperately jumped off on New Year's Eve. Nothing has a shorter life than a New Year's resolution, except, maybe, the hangover that usually goes along with it.

And we find ourselves in the middle of the bleak, cold, rainy month, watching summer on the airline commercials, with the turkey long gone, the tree taken down and the mailman arriving with the credit card statements. We haven't even the threat of roadside suspensions to excite us, just all those glittering, virtuous, self-improving promises littering our consciences like paper hats after a children's party.

January is the wrong month for a new year. New means shiny and fresh, pleasure and excitement. A different image (like new clothes), a different way of seeing (like new glasses), an unexperienced sense of wonder (like a new baby), and January, this month of short days and shorter tempers, has none of these.

Burns' Night comes in January, that strange non-holiday when the television stations dress their hosts in kilts, the newspapers reprint dubious recipes for haggis, and for one short day bagpipes are admitted to respectable society. But for the rest of us, the non-Scots, January is the saddest month, dull and grey of weather and, because of all those unfulfilled resolutions, a guilt-ridden month — nothing at all to do with the sort of feeling that comes with a new car, a new love, a new *anything*.

New Year's Day ideally should come in July, when the flowers are at their brightest, the leaves are on the trees and the fruits are promising to grow. Instead of the Polar Bears, those hearty masochists who leap into an icy ocean, shivering and blue (but not on the television), every man, woman, child and dog in the land could rush down the beach (say at noon on July 1) and come out warm in the sun to dry on the sand. That would be a good time to make resolutions, nice keepable resolutions, like "I will get more exercise, I will relax and take it easy, I will eat more fruit, get up early and lose ten pounds" — all of them sensible, workable, non-guilt resolutions which most

CABBAGE AND GARLIC SAUSAGE STEW

1 fresh green cabbage
1 garlic sausage or Ukrainian sausage
2 tbsp butter
1 bottle beer
caraway seeds
1 tsp ground pepper

Cut the sausage into bite sized chunks and the cabbage into thick slices. Melt butter and toss the cabbage for two minutes. Sprinkle with the pepper. Add the sausage, stir well and pour in half a bottle of beer.

Simmer, lid on, for two minutes, sprinkle generously with caraway seeds, stir and serve with fresh bread.

LEEK AND POTATO SOUP

2 potatoes, unpeeled and diced
2 - 3 leeks, halved lengthwise and thinly sliced
1 medium onion, finely chopped
2 tbsp oil
1/2 litre milk or coffee cream, or 1/2 cup heavy cream
1/2 tsp salt
1/2 tsp pepper
1/2 tsp ground nutmeg

Heat the oil and stir in the onion for two minutes. Add the leeks and stir another 2 minutes. Add the potatoes, stir again. Add the pepper, salt, nutmeg and enough hot water to cover it all. Simmer 30 minutes, stirring occasionally. Add the milk or cream, stir well and serve immediately.

For elegance, put the soup through a blender or processor before adding the cream.

VICHYSSOISE

Process the finished soup very smooth and chill.

of us could keep right through to October. We could then go into winter feeling good about ourselves, an approach the psychologists call "behavior modification by positive reinforcement," which means, in simple terms, that people like to do what they like to do.

But July 1 is already taken, and there's not much hope, under any government, of Canada Day trading places with New Year's. So we're stuck with it in January, and the only sensible thing to do, to make it bearable, is to make different resolutions. No more vague promises to "save money," but real winter resolutions like "I will eat more beans," or "I will make more stew," "I will learn to make bread, or dumplings. I will make big fat nourishing soups out of cheap ingredients, and I will even learn to make hotcakes for Saturday breakfast without opening a packet."

Each and every one of these promises is a money saver, but more important still, a time *user.* Saving time is a North American disease — we save time to be able to waste time watching television, we save time making odorless instant coffee when we all know that the real pleasure of coffee comes from the smell of it, and the sound of it perking and snuffling on the stove. I get people out of bed in my house by sprinkling coffee on the burners and turning them to low. In five minutes the heaviest sleepers, the snorters, the heads-below-the-pillowers and even the sleep-till-nooners are all up, noses twitching like beagles, expecting something. Real estate people all know that the way to sell a house is to bake cookies, or have bread in the oven — "makes it feel like home," they say, just as they say that a white picket fence around almost any old bit of scrub acreage will make the buyer feel like a real farmer.

When I cook at trade shows and shopping malls the P.A. system makes announcements, but nobody pays much attention. The first thing I do is cut up an onion and fry it. Instant crowd. People follow their noses like dogs to a bone. We forget that our houses should not only look like home, but smell like it. I have a recipe for chicken that is ridiculously simple, and takes hardly anytime at all, but its great advantage is that you can leave an empty house, go out and about, enjoy yourself, shop or do those time-saving things (even go to work) and come home to a kitchen that smells as if somebody actually *lived* in it, a kitchen warm with the aroma of roasting chicken, a house which almost reaches out to hug you and say, "I'm glad you're here, you're just in time for supper."

The trick is to turn the oven to 170° or 180°F, which hardly registers at all on the thermostat. Rub the chicken (and this recipe works well with the cheapest, most unassuming and ancient fowl you can find) with butter and pepper and salt. Set it in the roasting pan, surround it with a half dozen unpeeled whole medium-sized onions, and three or four unpeeled potatoes. This will take almost all of a minute. Crinkle some foil, and lay it over top of the chicken. Don't tuck it in, just let it be loose. Put the whole thing in the oven and go out. Trust me. When you come home five, six or even eight hours later, the house will be fully furnished — your nose will tell you. Whip off the foil, turn the oven up to 400°F for ten minutes (this crisps and browns the skin), and serve dinner with that terribly smug look of competence on your face. The onions squeeze out of their skins like toothpaste, the potatoes are floury inside (and welcome a pat of butter), and if you're energetic you can use the ten minutes at 400°F to make a salad.

Leeks are cheap in winter — good big leeks with long white stems. three leeks and two big potatoes will make a wonderful soup (add pepper, salt and nutmeg). Fancy restaurants muck about with just this soup, add a little cream and call it *vichyssoise,* but it doesn't have to go into the food processor or be sieved; it tastes even better with lumps in it. And although you won't find it in any cookbook, it is spectacular with Polish sausage (or any other smoky meat) cut up into rings and cooked with it.

When I lived in construction camps, where the rule was that men got as much to eat as they could hold and a bit extra, we ate in expensive and extravagant style — three or four steaks per man per meal, two or three pounds of chicken apiece, and lamb chops by the dozen. It was 20 below, and we all worked 14 hours a day. But despite all this indulgence, the favorite meal was garlic sausage and cabbage — everybody loved it, because it was (and still is) the cheapest and easiest of all simple suppers.

Slice a big shiny green cabbage into wedges, cut up an onion or two, and slice a big garlic sausage into half-inch rounds. Melt a lump of butter in a big pot, fry the onion a couple of minutes, throw in the cabbage and toss it all about to coat it well with butter, add the garlic sausage, a little salt, a lot of pepper and a healthy sprinkling of caraway seeds. Put the lid on and let it cook for half an hour to an hour. Serve it with rye bread or plain boiled potatoes, and if you want to make a social occasion of supper, buy a six-pack and pour in half a bottle when you add the sausage.

Virtue is a concept almost as old-fashioned today as chastity, partly because it is always associated with restraint, or being good by holding back. But there is a different kind of virtue, the kind that children know about, the feeling of self-worth and happiness that comes from purely personal achievement. The kitchen is just about the only place in the house where a whole family can re-learn this kind of virtue, where there is comfort, joy and enormous pleasure in doing something simple together, and then enjoying it together. The joy and the pleasure get mentioned in a lot of cookbooks, but comfort very infrequently, and almost never in New Year's resolutions.

CALDO VERDE

Cook as for leek and potato soup, substituting a few slices of chopped bacon for the oil, or add some ham, or use chicken stock instead of water. Chop a bunch of kale and add just after adding the potatoes.

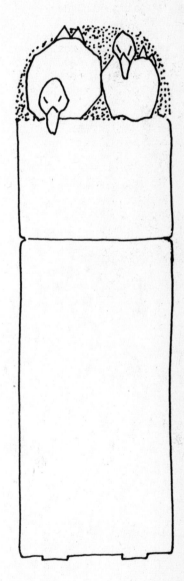

Hey, Good Lookin'...

how's about cookin' something up
with me?

"I love my Mom," in crayon, on a recycled paper plate — that's a
real Valentine, a little jam around the edges and the pink heart unstuck
and lost somewhere in the lunch box.

The rest of Valentine's Day has lost its innocence. I looked at a rack
of Valentines last week. There were Valentines for the boss, Valentines
for mothers-in-law, for "My favorite uncle," even for "The Best Dog
in The World." Some were sloppy: "Roses are Red...," some were
"smart:" "I'd honk my horn at you anytime;" and some were downright
cruel: "If you sat in my lap I'd die, you're so fat."

And the chocolates. Great heart-shaped boxes soft-centred with
calories and indigestion. I buy flowers. Daffodils are in season in
February. The closed ones sometimes take two days to open, and the
process is strangely exciting, like a very slow painting happening, a
bit more each time you look. But if you want instant color, put them
in lukewarm water. (They just won't last as long.)

Then there are all those recipes for Valentine's Day, with cream and
icing and fancy booze, with cherries and oysters and artichokes —
all the aphrodisiacs, the fancy foods that are supposed to put a high
gloss on your love life.

Most of them, however, in combination, will just give you a sleepless
night. Foods for lovers should be light, digestible, and easy on the pots
and pans. Nothing will stop the early stage of true love quicker than
a mountain of dishes; conversely, there is something particularly
bewitching in watching somebody make dinner in less than half an
hour.

Asparagus is a good place to start this kind of dinner. You don't need
a lot — half a pound is enough for two if it's fresh and crisp and the
bottom ends aren't wrinkled. Bend the stalks in your fingers until they
snap an inch or two from the bottom, wash them under the tap and
they're ready to cook. While you're shopping, buy a couple of lemons,
a few mushrooms, and a deboned and skinned chicken breast.

What we're going to cook is an Italian dish, called *Piccata di Vitello,*
which is usually made with veal. But we're going to use chicken, so
we'll call it *Piccata di Pollo.* It's ridiculously easy, an absolutely

foolproof, even idiot proof recipe, which takes five minutes to get ready and four to cook. It's pretty, and a very intimate thing to make, because you can't do it for four — it's a two people dish.

The best pot to cook asparagus in is an old coffee pot, without the basket and with a couple of inches of water in the bottom. Get it ready.

If you're going to eat rice with this, then put the rice on: two cups of water, one cup of rice, a little salt, bring it to the boil, turn the heat to the lowest and leave it covered (no stirring) for 20 minutes. If you put half a teaspoon of tumeric in the water at the beginning the rice will turn a brilliant yellow; and if you lift up the lid when it's cooked, throw in a handful of frozen peas and put the lid back while you cook the chicken, you'll have something very springlike — a perfect complement to the daffodils.

Now the chicken. Nine minutes total, even if you're slow. Dust each half of the breast with flour, and shake off the excess. Put each half between two sheets of waxed paper and lightly pound them (I use the side of a wine bottle) until they've spread to double their original size. Peel off the paper, and sprinkle them with pepper and salt. They're ready.

Put the coffee pot on to boil, and as soon as it does slide in the asparagus, butt ends down. Sprinkle them with salt, put the lid on and cook for exactly six minutes, after which you pour off the water (coffee pots are designed to do this with the lid on), tip the asparagus onto a plate, and put a slice of butter on it to melt.

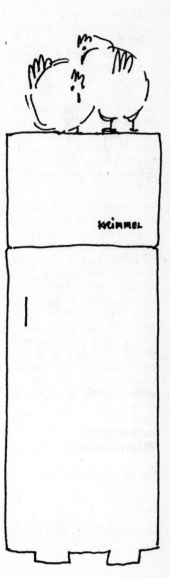

Back to the chicken. Melt a tablespoon of butter in a frypan over medium heat (an electric frypan works well too, set at 325°F). Lay in the chicken, and cook for one minute (the edge of the breast will turn white). Now turn it over, and cook another minute. Pour in half a cup of white wine, dry cider or apple juice, sprinkle with tarragon, cook one minute more, turning once, and take the chicken out. Squeeze in the juice of half a lemon, and boil (high heat) for one minute. That's the sauce. Pour it over the chicken (a piece on each plate), add the rice, decorate it with asparagus and dinner's ready, a Valentine's dinner, bright green shiny asparagus, golden rice to match the daffodils, and the chicken, the *Piccata di Pollo,* which nobody can make any better than you, and a candle on the table.

I think that's a lot better than candy. The mushrooms? An hour before dinner I put them in a screw-top jar, sprinkle them with a little salt and pepper, add three tablespoons of olive oil, the juice of the spare lemon half and four or five pinches of tarragon or thyme. I shake the jar well, and leave it an hour. They come out white and shiny, crisp and fresh-tasting — a simple appetizer.

And dessert? Peel a ripe avocado, mash it with two tablespoons of sugar or honey, the juice of the remaining lemon and half a teaspoon of instant coffee. You can do it in the blender very quickly. Now add

AVOCADO DESSERT

1 peeled avocado
2 tbsp sugar or honey
juice of half a lemon
1/2 tsp instant coffee

Mash or blend all the ingredients together. Add an equal amount of vanilla ice-cream, mix well and put into wine glasses. Freeze for half an hour or until just stiff.

PICCATA DI POLLO

1 chicken breast
1/2 cup white wine, dry cider or apple juice
juice of half a lemon
1 tbsp butter
tarragon

Dust the chicken breast with flour, shaking off the excess. Lightly pound each half between waxed paper until they have doubled in size. Sprinkle them with pepper and salt.

Melt the butter in a frypan over medium heat. Lay in the chicken and cook for one minute (the edge of the breast will turn white). Turn it over and cook another minute. Pour in the white wine, dry cider or apple juice, sprinkle with tarragon and cook another minute, turning once. Remove the chicken and add the lemon juice. Boil over high heat for another minute. Pour this sauce over the chicken and serve.

MARINATED MUSHROOMS

See Page 41 for recipe.

an equal amount of vanilla ice cream, mix it well, put it in wine glasses and freeze for half an hour, so it's just stiff. This is enough for four, because it's very rich and because nobody sells half avocados.

In Praise Of Peanut Butter

Add a dash to your cooking . . . but don't tell anyone.

Polite society is really a collection of words that people don't say. Politicians, no matter how deceptive or dishonest their actions may prove them to be, may not be called barefaced liars, just as teenagers who resolutely do nothing may not be described as idle. Making peace with your neighbor's dog is not achieved by a phone call about "that yapping pooch," and the overweight are never fat, but plump, chubby or, best of all, "comfortable."

All societies have their special language of words that are not said. A Manitoba judge recently decided that THE word is permissible, and that policemen must accept it as part of a polite request for them to go away. But television stations still resolutely bleep it out, families still don't accept it as a conventional farewell, and even cats, normally the most placid and philosophical of animals, tend to look offended at its use. Doctors, lawyers (particularly lawyers), psychologists, fashion writers, realtors and car salesmen have all made structured lives and comfortable incomes by refusing to call a spade a spade, referring instead to a primary agricultural instrument.

The gourmets, too, are heavily involved in denying simplicity. A stew is no more a stew, but a *ragout.* Nothing is fried, although much is *sautéed,* knives become *hachoirs* and cooks don't exist anymore — they have to be "chefs." Vegetables have stopped being crisp, a simple, direct and honest state for them, but almost invariably are "al dente."

Wine is never simply described as "a good drinking wine," but is slurped, sucked, sloshed around in glasses, peered through in candlelight, frowned over and discussed. Anybody crass enough to say "plonk" out loud in wine circles is almost 100 percent sure of not getting invited back.

Food and drink, the most common, frequent and satisfying sources of our basic lusts and passions, are rapidly becoming elitist exercises in specialist equipment, using a complicated vocabulary. Nobody tells you that an ordinary bread knife is the best tool for slicing tomatoes, or that an empty spice jar, shaken by hand, makes salad dressings quicker than any complicated machinery. You can say "screw top

PEANUT BUTTER SAUCE

2 tbsp peanut butter
2 cloves garlic, finely
chopped
juice of a medium-sized
lemon
yoghurt

*Stir together the peanut
butter, garlic and lemon
juice. Add equal amount of
plain yoghurt and stir until it
has a creamy consistency.*

*Serve sauce on roast lamb
or steamed broccoli.*

PEANUT BUTTER DIP

*Divide peanut butter sauce
into three bowls. Add half a
teaspoon of curry powder to
one, a good pinch of
cayenne pepper to another
and leave one plain. Serve
with raw vegetables and
crusty bread.*

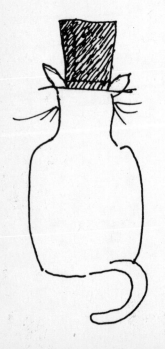

container" around gourmets, but never "jam jar."

Peanut butter is another dirty word in high-class kitchens. Cheap, basic, probably the most popular of all childhood foods, peanut butter goes on sandwiches, with jelly or bananas. We discuss it in highly emotional terms like "crunchy's better — no, it isn't — yes, it is," or we sit in strange places and lust after it (I was once in northern Japan, quite happy to have lived on fish for three months, but conscious of some basic lack in my life). Peanut butter is comfort, warmth, security and home; it's memories of sucking it out of your teeth, or licking a bit stuck to the roof of your mouth. We write eulogies to sandlot baseball, to fishing holes and fishing poles, and we give Canada Council grants to preserve our memories of little red schoolhouses. But nobody writes poems to peanut butter. Or recipes. Peanut butter cookies crop up almost shamefacedly, but in all the 420 pages of my *Joy of Cooking,* that's the only reference to our national food.

I recently came across a gourmet recipe for Ghanian Chicken ("delight and surprise your friends with this unusual dish"). It seriously suggested that to cook it, one pound of peanuts should be purchased, that they should be blanched in boiling water, skinned, dried, and then roasted carefully in a 250°F oven for 30 minutes, after which, by using a mortar and pestle or a food processor, they should be reduced to a "smooth, homogenous paste" which then, to "remove any unprocessed lumps," should "be forced through a fine sieve." The end result of this process, which takes up three hours of your life and dirties up half a dozen dishes, is peanut butter, pure and simple, but the recipe goes on to talk about "the paste."

We, however, even though I may get expelled from the International Gourmet Sociey, are going to deal with peanut butter, which is always on hand. Dump your prejudices, let your curiosity take over, try some of these ideas and cultivate that smug, virtuous smile which comes from brand new ideas.

Tahini, which is basically ground sesame seeds, appears in large numbers of Greek and Middle Eastern cookbooks. It is usually very expensive, and goes rancid very quickly. In most recipes calling for tahini, peanut butter can be substituted.

Take two tablespoons of peanut butter and stir into it with a fork two cloves of finely chopped garlic. Now add the juice of a medium-sized lemon, and stir that in. As you stir it will get thicker. Now stir in about the same quantity of plain yogurt, until it all has a creamy consistency. You can now use it for a sauce with plain baked lamb, steamed broccoli, or thinned out (with more yogurt) as a wonderful salad dressing. You can serve it as a dip with raw vegetables and chunks of crusty bread, and if you want to be a generous host then divide it into three bowls, add half a teaspoon of curry powder to one, a good pinch of red cayenne pepper to another, and leave one as is. This is the simplest of all things to do with peanut butter (except spreading it on bread), and is a good way to get used to the idea of using it in cooking.

Next time you're going to roast lamb, follow your favorite recipe for cooking times, but before putting it in the oven make shallow cuts in a diamond pattern, then spread the top surface with a mixture of peanut butter, garlic and lemon juice, diluted down to spreading consistency with a little water. Rub it into the cuts, and let it cook. If you want a really dark, crispy looking lamb, sprinkle a little sugar over it 20 minutes before it's finished. Serve it with lemon quarters on each plate.

If you're going to broil lamb chops (or even hamburgers), spread some peanut butter on them, thinned out a little with water and spiced up with hot red pepper. And if you want to make a wonderful African-style stew for two or three people, try this:

Fry one pound of pork shoulder, cut into cubes, in a tablespoon of oil until the outsides are light brown. Push it all to the sides of the pan, and fry half an onion, cut very fine, until it is light brown and starting to smell like fried onion. Add two cloves of garlic, chopped coarse, then stir the meat and onions all together. Push it all aside again, and add 2 tablespoons of peanut butter, ½ teaspoon salt, a good pinch of red pepper (cayenne) and half to three-quarters of a cup of water, chicken stock, white wine or beer — whichever you have handy. Stir it all into a sauce and add one-and-a-half onions cut into largish chunks. Stir it all together again and spread it evenly over the bottom of the pan. Now lay over the top fresh broccoli cut into flowerets, fresh green beans in finger lengths, quartered tomatoes, red or green bell peppers cut in chunks — any nice, fresh, colourful and preferably inexpensive vegetable you can find — sprinkle a little salt over all (that keeps in the color), put the lid on and let cook over low/medium heat for ten minutes. Toss it all together just before serving, and next time do the same thing with chicken wings. Or bits of lamb.

Just don't tell too many people what you're doing or the price of peanut butter will go up.

PORK AND PEANUT BUTTER AFRICAN-STYLE

1 lb pork shoulder, cubed
2 onions, finely chopped
1 tbsp oil
2 cloves garlic, coarsely chopped
2 tbsp peanut butter
1/2 tsp salt
a good pinch of cayenne pepper
1/2 - 3/4 cup water, chicken stock, white wine or beer
broccoli, cut into florets
green beans, cut into finger lengths
tomatoes, quartered
red or green bell peppers, cut in chunks

Fry the cubed pork in the oil until it is light brown. Push to the sides of the pan and fry half an onion, until light brown.

Add the coarsely chopped garlic, then stir the meat and onions all together. Push aside again and add the peanut butter, salt, cayenne pepper and the water, chicken stock, white wine or beer. Stir into a sauce and add the rest of the onions.

Stir and spread evenly over the bottom of the pan. Lay the vegetables over the top (and any vegetables you may have), sprinkle with salt to keep in the colour, put the lid on and cook over low/medium heat for ten minutes. Toss all together just before serving.

Try chicken wings instead of the pork or bits of lamb.

Garlic
The Barely Respectable Bulb.

Garlic scares away vampires in Transylvania and on late-night television. It keeps away evil spirits in Greece and in the whole continent of India; it cures colds in Russia and, eaten raw in sandwiches, it nourishes Belgian peasants. It makes Japanese women fertile, Latin-American men potent, young children the world over immune to viruses and the tired blood of old men quicken in their veins.

But in the English-speaking world, garlic is barely respectable. It's a guaranteed laugh for a stand-up comic, a horror movie to teenagers, "something we don't really talk about" in polite society and a full-blown nightmare to salesmen, advertising executives and anybody else who talks, face to face, to anybody else for a living. I once convinced a perfectly nice, not-too-bright but not totally stupid friend of mine that I could smell last night's garlic on his breath. We were talking on the phone.

Children can graduate from high school after years of Home Ec. never having been taught that garlic is just about the single most important thing they will find in their kitchen. Home economists, most of whom don't like food and certainly don't like cooking, encourage children, senior citizens, hospital patients, airline passengers and everybody else in their captive audiences to believe in the myth of garlic, the anti-social boogieman which hides in the corners of "foreign foods" awaiting its chance to make the world reject you.

Smokers, reeking of stale tobacco, their fingers yellow to the wrist and their hair needing to be steam-cleaned, will piously and cross-eyed tell you that they couldn't eat anything with garlic in it — they can't stand the smell.

Gourmet magazines, which are the *Playboys* of the food business (a more valid comparison than I originally thought, with all the faked-up centrefolds of unattainable glamour and the purple prose describing what ought to be a perfectly normal experience), go so far as to recommend that you wear rubber gloves to handle garlic — a suggestion almost as silly as wearing a raincoat to play football.

Food is a natural, organic experience, not an exercise in household hygiene. Everything we eat grows in the ground or on the ground. Our lives really consist of coming to terms with various aspects of nature — dirt, colour, smells, untidiness, even unhappiness. And the more we try to avoid the reality of nature the more trouble we have. Psychiatrists get rich showing us the things we are determined not to see, lawyers prosper on the divorces which spring from evading simple issues, and the rest of us let ourselves be conned into thinking that we should all live our lives like the Man From Glad, sterile and immaculate, using only one of our senses, the one which tells us when something *looks* nice.

Touch, smell and sound we learn to appreciate only in synthetic form. Tape-recorded bird songs finish up being more popular than the real thing, kids practice for lip-synch competitions because we won't, or don't want to, listen to the reality of their own human, imperfect but non-electronic voices. And garlic comes in little jars, powdered and sanitized, so that we don't have to touch it.

The easiest way to handle garlic is on a chopping board, nice fresh garlic, shiny and white and plump. When you buy it, feel it. If it's soft or dry or musty, go elsewhere. Don't buy garlic in packets; buy it loose and look for the same signs of health as you look for in other vegetables — the sort of vigor and liveliness that you see on healthy babies. Store it in a cool place, not in the dark and not in the refrigerator, or it will think it is spring and time to start sprouting. A little wicker basket is fine, or one of those ceramic garlic keepers — anything to let the air circulate around it. Squash each clove with the side of a knife, and if it is fresh the skin will pop so that you can shake the clove loose without ever touching the garlic itself. Chop it and scoop it up with the knife — that's a lot easier than getting out the garlic press and having to pick the bits out of the holes with a toothpick.

If you want to get the smell of garlic off your fingers, run them under the cold tap, which will wash the oil off. The hot tap will open your pores and let it seep in.

But one of the nicest ways of cooking garlic is without peeling it at all. Whole cloves, still in their white skins and dropped into a stew, give a very soft, gentle flavour of cut or chopped garlic. And if you do have fussy guests, who demand to know "Is there any garlic in this?," then just before your dish goes to the table you fish them out (the cloves, not the guests) and smile your most reassuring smile (the one you learn from children, the "not me" smile) and say, "No, no garlic."

Everybody has heard of the 40 cloves of garlic recipe, and very few dare to try it. This again is so simple — three or four heads of garlic, broken up into cloves, not peeled, but scattered over the bottom of a roasting pan. Take a three- or four-pound fryer, rub it with a little salt and pepper and a little olive oil, poke holes all over the skin of

CHICKEN AND FORTY CLOVES OF GARLIC

3 - 4 lb frying chicken
1 lemon
3 - 4 heads of garlic

Break up the garlic into cloves, without peeling, and scatter them over the bottom of a roasting pan. Rub the chicken with a little salt, pepper and olive oil. Poke holes over the skin of the lemon with a skewer and place in chicken.

Place the chicken on top of the garlic and put in oven pre-heated to 400°F. Roast for about an hour. Remove chicken and place on one side to set.

Pour the pan juices into a cup, allow fat to rise (about 5 minutes), spoon off and serve the sauce with the chicken. Or, return the juices to the pan, bring to a boil, add a cup of red wine or beer and boil down by half. Serve with chicken.

GARLIC BREAD

2 sticks of butter
4 cloves of garlic

Melt the butter, add the chopped garlic and cook over low heat for ten minutes. Strain it through muslin and keep in fridge. Spread on bread and warm in the oven.

GARLIC OIL

6 cloves of garlic
bottle of peanut or olive oil

Chop the garlic and leave in the bottle of oil for three to four days. Strain and use.

a juicy lemon with a skewer, and put the lemon in the chicken. Set the chicken on the garlic, and put it into an oven pre-heated to 400°F.

In an hour's time, the skin will be crisp and golden, the meat will be juicy, and the bottom of the roasting pan will be filled with roasted garlic cloves, chicken fat and lemon juice. Put the chicken on one side to set, tell the kids to set the table, your spouse to light the candles, while you take out the garlic cloves with a slotted spoon and arrange them around the chicken. Pour the pan juices into a cup, let the fat rise to the top (about five minutes) and spoon it off. Without any further treatment this is a wonderful and fragrant sauce, but if you put it back in the pan, bring it to a boil, add a cup of red wine or beer, and boil it down by half you will have something quite extraordinary.

The first clove of garlic you eat requires a small amount of courage. Hold it between your first finger and thumb, take it to your mouth and press. The inside will squeeze out like toothpaste and, strangely, it will not taste like garlic at all, but more like a roast chestnut. And because it has not been cut it will have almost no smell. In Spain, people squeeze the roasted garlic out of the skins and spread it on good bread, then pepper it well.

If you're going to chop your garlic and fry it, put it in the pan when the onions are almost cooked. Garlic is fragile, and it burns easily. Or melt two sticks of butter, add four chives of chopped garlic, and let it cook on low heat for ten minutes. Strain it through muslin, and keep it in the fridge, ready to butter a little bread which can warm in the oven while you cook a hamburger — instant garlic bread — or to sauté a few vegetables in.

I make garlic oil by chopping half a dozen cloves of garlic and leaving them in a bottle of peanut or olive oil for three or four days. Strain it, and it's instantly ready, no fuss. Life just gets a little better and you don't really know why.

Apart from all the pleasures, it's good for you. Chicken soup is not called Jewish penicillin for nothing — no grandmother would dream of making chicken soup without garlic. A recent University of Chicago study proved that garlic was an efficient cold remedy, and cholesterol melts away when regularly treated to fresh garlic.

If you're still worried about your social life, fresh-squeezed orange juice, really fresh, do it yourself, is a very efficient remedy, and so is fresh parsley, chewed a couple of minutes, but best of all is something the southern Italians and the northern Japanese share. They take leaves of fresh mint, wrapped around their forefinger, and rub their teeth with them.

And strangely enough, if you make a really hot, spicy, garlicky chile, and at the last moment add either a spoonful of dry mint or a dozen or so chopped fresh mint leaves, not only does the flavor enormously improve, but there is almost no residual aroma.

Warming Up To Summer

Nothing stops the dedicated barbecuer.

Sometimes summer forgets to happen. We each write our individual scripts for long soft sunny days, for longer and lazy evenings, for beaches and bonfires, bikinis, backyard tans and busy bumblebees (only the bumblebees). But the June brides, the Little Leaguers, the company picnics, even the humblest of backyard barbecues, have all been rained on (if not drowned out), and the great sun-warmed outdoors of the soft drink commercials never seems to mention the days when the World Congress of Mosquitos holds its own picnic in your backyard.

B.C. summers are a gamble. The sun works a five-day week, "No Saturdays, maybe a couple of hours on Sunday, lemme think about it, don't bug me." So we move the party to the kitchen but the hamburgers aren't the same under the broiler, the garlic bread tastes funny and Fred's shorts — so dashing on the patio — suddenly look like garage sale specials, or props for a silent movie. Moving an outside party is seldom successful, but an inside party — a few nice, simple easy things — can easily go out into the sun if and when it decides to come out.

The trick is to keep it simple. Most of the really great dishes of the world started off as one-pot meals, made in a hurry by a woman who didn't have much of either time nor money. Travellers ate these dishes, came home and raved about them, fancied them up and made them difficult, expensive and complicated.

Bouillabaisse used to be a nice, simple fish stew, made by the fishermen's wives out of fish their husbands couldn't sell, because it was ugly, or battered, or because none of the regular customers felt like fish that day. Today there is hardly a recipe for bouillabaisse which doesn't include prawns (at $12 a pound), lobster, crab, clams and mussels, and this one-time cheap dish ends up needing a bank loan to get it on the table.

In Spain and Portugal paella is not such a big deal, but simply outdoor picnic food, — the Iberian equivalent of our barbecue. Families go out into the country with their paella pan, a box of matches, some rice, a chicken and a little twist of saffron. North

SUPER-STICKY BARBECUE SAUCE

1 cup sugar
1 cup vinegar
1 cup soy sauce
3 tbsp cornstarch
3 tbsp whiskey (or rum or vodka)
1/2 tsp cayenne pepper

Bring the sugar, vinegar and soy sauce to the boil. Mix the cornstarch with the whiskey and cayenne pepper. Pour the cornstarch into the sugar mixture, and boil, on medium heat, until it is glossy and coats the spoon. Pour into a jar, let it cool, cover and refrigerate until needed.

TERIYAKI CHICKEN WINGS

4 - 5 lb chicken wings
1/2 cup barbecue sauce (see above)
1 bottle of beer

Cut the wings, through the joints, into three pieces. The end bits put into a pot of boiling water for a future chicken stock. Marinate the remainder in the barbecue sauce diluted with the beer. They can marinate, stirred occasionally, for several hours.

Remove from the marinade, brush with a little undiluted barbecue sauce and place straight on the barbecue or bake in a 400°F oven for 20 minutes.

American paella recipes go on for pages, and the shopping takes longer than the eating.

The "one-pot" cooks are the real artists of summer cooking. The rest of us, with out gold-plated corn holders, porcelain butter warmers, Steuben finger bowls, and nuclear-powered martini chillers are simply slaves to fashion. But summer fashion, as the bikini so dramatically demonstrates, is most successful when it's minimal.

So let's concentrate on how little we can do to make summer supper. If the sun shines, fine, we'll use the barbecue for everything: steaks, hamburgers, chicken and corn. But let's not spend a lot of time picking the silk out of the stripped ears of corn before we wrap it in foil. Instead, put all the corn, with the husks still on it, in a bucket of cold water and leave it for half an hour while the barbecue heats up. Then just throw the corn on the grill, turn it occasionally, and let it cook in its own skin. The corn husks will turn brown and finally black, but the inside, the corn itself, will be moist and a little smoky, with a big flavour of fresh corn which seems to be concentrated in the silk and the husks. Like all barbecued food, it takes a little while to discover the right cooking time, but it's about the same as when the corn is in foil.

Then there's the barbecue sauce, which, whether you buy it in the bottle or make yourself, always seems to slide off the meat while it's cooking, requiring continual dabbing and brushing and producing that familiar aroma of singed wrist hair.

I make a barbecue basting sauce that sticks. It's simple and inexpensive, keeps well, and develops a nice shiny glossiness which gets into all the corners and crevices of whatever it is you're barbecuing. Make a big jar at the beginning of summer (or a number of smaller jars which you can give to your friends, smiling modestly ". . . actually it's a secret recipe handed down from some people who actually knew Joan of Arc quite well.") There's another chore dispensed with, another pan you don't have to mess with, and not only do you have almost instant teriyaki chicken wings — just brush them well and bake in 400°F oven for 20 minutes.

Chicken wings are probably the ideal indoor/outdoor barbecue solution. I buy four to five pounds, cut them through the joints into three pieces, and put the skinny end bits into a pot of boiling water for a little stock.

The remainder I put to marinate in half a cup of barbecue sauce diluted with a bottle of beer. They can sit in it for hours; just stir them occasionally. When enough people have arrived, and if the weather is fine, the wings go straight on the barbecue, brushed with a little undiluted barbecue sauce. You know how to do that. But if you're going to be indoors, try this Orientalized version of a famous Spanish dish, arroz con pollo, or simply chicken with rice. It looks spectacular piled up on the biggest dish you have in the middle of the table; it takes at most 30 minutes to make, and it is one of those dishes that seems to have been invented to go with inexpensive red wine. Marinate the chicken wings in the barbecue sauce for an hour or two.

Put the rice, water, turmeric and salt into a large saucepan, bring it to a boil over high heat, and immediately reduce heat to lowest, cover and let cook for 20 minutes. Meanwhile, in your largest, heaviest frypan (an electric pan will do fine), heat the oil, remove the chicken wings from the marinade and fry them on both sides (about ten minutes in all). Mix the pepper well with the onion, add to the pan and stir it around the chicken wings. Cook uncovered, stirring occasionally, for ten minutes, adding the thyme and garlic after five minutes.

Stir in the peas, still frozen, and cook for two minutes more. Take the lid off the rice, leave for two minutes over low heat to dry a little, and pile it on a big dish. Dump the chicken wings onto the rice, sprinkle the whole thing with parsley and stand back for applause.

If you want to be even fancier, and give supper a more Oriental flavour, fried bananas (cut in half lengthwise, and fried 3 to 4 minutes in a little butter, then sprinkled with cinnamon) go very well with this dish. So do flaked almonds, fried in a little butter or roasted peanuts crushed with a rolling pin. Steamed asparagus or green beans look wonderful around the rim of the dish, but you don't need to go much further than the basics. Kitchen reputations are best built on these simplicities.

CHICKEN WINGS ORIENTAL

18 chicken wings, cut into sections
1 cup barbecue sauce
1 bottle beer
2 cups rice
1 tsp salt
4 cups water
1 tsp turmeric
3 tbsp oil (olive, peanut or safflower)
1 large onion, finely chopped
1/2 tsp pepper
2 cloves garlic, chopped fine
1/2 tsp dried thyme
1 packet frozen peas
1/2 bunch parsley, chopped fine

Marinate the chicken pieces in the barbecue sauce and beer for an hour or two. Put the rice, water, turmeric and salt into large pan, bring to boil over high heat, reduce heat to lowest, cover and let cook for 20 minutes.

Heat the oil in your largest, heaviest frypan and fry the chicken wings on both sides (about 10 minutes). Mix the pepper and onion well, add to the pan and stir with the chicken wings. Cook uncovered, stirring occasionally, for 10 minutes, adding the thyme and garlic after 5 minutes. Stir in the peas (still frozen) and cook for further 2 minutes. Remove lid from the rice and leave for 2 minutes to dry a little, then pile it on a big dish. Dump chicken wings over the rice, sprinkle with parsley and serve.

For a more Oriental touch, cut bananas lengthwise and fry for 3 - 4 minutes in some butter, then sprinkle with cinnamon. Or fry flaked almonds in a little butter or crush some roasted peanuts.

The Watched Pot

Sometimes good cooking is not what you do, it's what you don't do.

CHICKEN STOCK

3-4 lb chicken backs or
necks or one boiling fowl
2 sticks of celery
1 onion, quartered
1 carrot, chopped
1 bay leaf
8 cups of water

Bring all the ingredients to a boil and simmer for 2 hours. Strain, cool and keep in the freezer in 2-cup containers.

Nobody can tell anybody else how to cook rice. The basics are simple: a pot with a lid and about twice as much water as rice. But the pot can be a tin can in the woods, a saucepan on the stove or a casserole in the oven; it can be a Japanese steamer or a Chinese wok, and the rice can be wrapped in a cloth or even in a lotus leaf. The water can be three times as much, even four, and it need not even be water. It can be chicken stock, milk, vegetable water — even beer. You can use almost any kind of liquid so long as it's wet.

And that's just for simple rice. There are the rice puddings of our childhood, some hated and some desperately remembered; there are the rice puddings of Greece and Persia and Germany — from wherever your grandmother called home — and there are Parsi weddings with rice wrapped in banana leaves.

Chinese grandmothers sit for hours stirring *congee,* a thick porridge of rice boiled slowly to a chewy sludge. Babies are fed it straight, and everybody else gets little bits of fish or meat dropped in it. Even today, in well-fed North America, there is an enormous following for *congee* in the Chinese community, among both the young and old, and strange though it may seem, an increasing number of Occidentals consider it to be something very special.

Rice is addictive. When I came home from my first trip to Japan, I was eating four or five bowls a day. Breakfast, lunch and dinner. I still eat a lot of rice, and look with despair at the people who pour soya sauce on it. There is a lot to be learned from simple, plain rice, properly cooked and eaten as a foil, a contrast, to the more flavourful cooked foods that it is usually served with. Rice, to Orientals, is more than just food: it is life and survival and a religion. There is something very impressive when, at the end of a meal, an old man puts a spoonful of rice in a bowl, adds a little tea, drinks it all and quietly nods. "To remind him of when there was nothing else to eat but a few grains of rice and some tea," says his grandson. Nobody smiles.

But holy and wonderful and satisfying as plain rice may be, there are some lovely dishes to be cooked with it, and the best of them all are the simplest — they just take time. And as you may be discovering from this series of stories, I'm very much taken with time as an ingredient.

Cooking something slowly and meditatively is a luxury, and a perfect excuse for doing almost nothing, very carefully. I teach a class occasionally for heart attack survivors, most of them power trippers addicted to moving and shaking the affairs of the world. I teach them to make bread. Their doctors tell them it's for the exercise, and indeed there is a bit of muscle involved in the kneading. But the really interesting thing to watch is their coming to terms with doing nothing.

The bread won't rise in a hurry. Nothing will speed it up. After the second time, they realize that the longer it takes to rise the better bread it is, and so they have even longer to spend fully occupied with doing nothing. But there is nobody teaching breadmaking in medical school, and no chances to learn about the therapeutic virtues of stirring — just standing there, alone in time, with a wooden spoon in your hand. "Sometimes I sits and thinks," says the old joke, "and sometimes . . . I just sits."

The first, and most perfect, almost completely failsafe one-pot rice dish to learn is risotto, about which fancy cookbooks will caution you most excessively. Make it once and you're an expert, even to your in-laws. Make it twice and you'll know that blacks ain't got monopoly on soul food, and not on soul either. A good risotto is comfort and home, your mother's knee and a seat by the fire. It's a basic, ancient dish, a tradition in Italy which goes back to before Columbus, and it's best to buy Italian rice to make it — it's more absorbent, and the risotto will turn out the same way as it has in Italy for the last 400 years. Look for Arborio rice, which comes under all kinds of brand names. All over the packet will be written *Riso Superfino Arborio,* but there will be no cooking instructions. Most delicatessens or specialty food shops, and even the occasional supermarket, will have Arborio. It's worth the effort to find it, since this is a dish of which you are going to be enormously proud.

Chicken stock is easy. Just boil 3 or 4 pounds of backs or necks, even an old boiling fowl big enough to be called a stag, for a couple of hours with a stick or two of celery, a quartered onion, a bay leaf and a carrot (another excuse for doing nothing; just read a book while it simmers). Strain it all, let it cook, and keep it in the freezer in 2-cup containers.

Now, the risotto which is going to make your name and change your life. Put four tablespoons of nice salted butter, a medium onion chopped small and a half teaspoon of pepper in a heavy frypan, and cook gently on medium heat, stirring constantly, until the onion is transparent. Add two cups of Arborio rice and stir it into the onion, with the heat turned up a bit, until it has absorbed all the butter and you see the rice grains beginning to change colour. Lift it from the

RISOTTO

4 tbsp salted butter
1 medium onion, chopped small
1/2 tsp ground pepper
2 cups Arborio rice
6 cups chicken stock or 5 cups chicken stock and 1 cup of white wine

Fry the butter, onion and pepper in a heavy frypan until onion is transparent. Add rice and stir it into the onion with the heat increased. Stir until the rice has absorbed all the butter and the granules are starting to change colour. Lift it from the bottom as you stir, turning it over.

Pour in 1/2 cup of stock and stir. Reduce heat to medium/low. Slowly add the rest of the stock, 1/2 cup at a time and stirring slowly. Add the last cups very slowly to avoid turning the mixture into a mush - each grain of rice should be separate. Taste frequently. Put into a warm serving dish, sprinkle with grated Parmesan cheese and serve.

MUSHROOM RISOTTO

Make risotto as above but use 5 cups chicken stock and soak one packet of dried Italian mushrooms in one cup of white wine for half an hour.

Remove the mushrooms and slice 1/2 lb fresh mushrooms thin. Add both mushrooms after 15 minutes of cooking the rice plus 1/2 tsp salt and the soaking wine. Finish cooking, sprinkle with grated Parmesan cheese and serve.

RISOTTO MILANESE

Make risotto as above but use 5 cups chicken stock and soak a little saffron in one cup of white wine. Add it to the risotto after the third cup of stock, 1/2 cup at a time. Finish cooking, sprinkle with grated Parmesan cheese and serve.

RICE PUDDING

1 cup pearl rice (or medium grain)
6 cups milk
1/4 cup sugar
4 half-inch strips of lemon peel
1/2 tsp powdered cinnamon
3 whole cloves
2 eggs, well beaten
1 cup sultanas, soaked 30 minutes in sherry or rye

Put all the ingredients, except the eggs and sultanas, in a heavy-bottomed pan and bring to a boil over medium heat stirring occasionally. Turn down the heat and simmer, stirring occasionally, for 30 - 40 minutes until the rice is soft and everything has thickened. Add the sultanas and cook 5 minutes more.

Spoon 2 tbsp of the hot rice into the eggs, stir, add another 2 tbsp and stir, and once again. Add the egg mixture to the rice, stir it well and pour into dish. Allow to cool to room temperature, sprinkle the top with cinnamon and serve.

bottom as you stir, turning it over — exactly the right job for one of those square-ended wooden spatulas. At this moment the rice will also develop a nice, slightly nutty smell. Pour in half a cup of stock, and stir it in, slowly and contemplatively. When it is absorbed, another half cup, another stir. Don't rush it, enjoy it. Reduce the heat to medium/low. Another half cup. And so on to six cups. Rice varies in the amount of liquid it can absorb. Sometimes the whole six cups, sometimes five. So add a cup of wine, half a cup at a time, after the third cup of stock. Each grain of rice should be separate, slightly crunchy but very flavourful with the chicken stock which has become concentrated during the cooking. Add the last cups very slowly, in small amounts, because it mustn't turn into mush. Taste frequently the first time you make it, and you will know exactly when to stop. Put it into a warm serving dish, sprinkle with grated Parmesan cheese, and serve.

If you want to make a mushroom risotto, soak one packet of dried Italian mushrooms half an hour in the wine you're going to use for cooking. Then fish them out and chop them and slice ½ pound fresh mushrooms thin. Add both mushrooms after fifteen minutes of cooking the rice, together with ½ teaspoon salt and the soaking wine. Finish cooking, sprinkle generously with Parmesan, and serve.

If you want to spend money, buy a lot of Parmesan and a little saffron. Soak the saffron in the cooking wine, and add it as usual. This is a Risotto Milanese — no mushrooms, nothing but rice, stock, wine and saffron. Perfectly gorgeous. But make a simple risotto first, just to get the technique right.

Eggs and lemon are the basis of a great deal of Greek cooking. Rice pudding is another simple stirred dish, utterly simple to make, and soft, velvety and surprising to eat. It uses lots of milk, and can be eaten hot or cold. It will freeze and keep if you have any leftovers. *If.*

Put the rice and everything except the eggs and sultanas in a good heavy bottomed pan and bring to a boil over medium heat, stirring occasionally, for 30 to 40 minutes until the rice is soft and everything has thickened. Add the sultanas and cook five minutes more. Spoon 2 tablespoons of the hot rice into the eggs, stir well, add another 2 tablespoons and stir, once again. Now add the egg mixture to the rice, stir it well, and pour it into a serving dish or cups. Let cool to room temperature, and sprinkle the top with cinnamon. To be really self-indulgent, drizzle a little thick cream over each serving. Good food doesn't have to be complicated.

Home Grown Charm

It is possible to be too perfect?
Ask a strawberry.

Pretty girl, pretty girl, wilt thou be mine,
Thou shalt not wash dishes nor yet feed the swine
But sit on a cushion and sew a fine seam,
And dine upon strawberries, and sugar and cream.

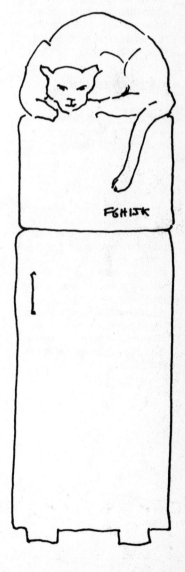

California strawberries look like strawberries, but they don't taste like anything very much. They rely on our memories for their appeal; they turn back our clocks to the one time that we ate a perfect, freshly picked, fully ripe strawberry, still warm from the sun and so dark red as to be almost black, so dripping with juice as to be a dry cleaner's delight. Fresh local strawberries are the essence of summer, an unassailable argument for local farming and for things picked fully ripe and eaten immediately. They are food in the true sense of the word, each strawberry a unique and unrepeatable command performance by God, the sun and the rain. The fresh strawberry, which is no relation at all to the frozen strawberry, and only very distantly recognizes its California cousin, is a joy and a wonder, a short-term passion of self-indulgence which, because it costs so little, frequently fails to achieve its full dignity.

This is one of the tragedies of seasonal and inexpensive food — somehow it doesn't seem worth making the same effort for local herrings as we do for imported shark. And fresh local mushrooms, which in France are called "Champignons de Paris" and sell for ten dollars a pound, we often overlook in favour of their more exotic, and much more expensive, competition.

But apart from the problem of being local and inexpensive, the strawberry also suffers from its perfection. What to do but eat them? Plain (if you must wash them then do it very quickly, and hull them later so that the water doesn't get in and dilute the flavour); or with cream (some like it whipped but I prefer it poured from a jug, and if you look around there is now a company producing local Jersey cream almost thick enough to walk on); with sour cream and brown sugar; with red wine (what a wonderful summer afternoon — two deck chairs, a seven dollar bordeaux, two pounds of strawberries and

STRAWBERRIES AND PEPPER

strawberries
coarsely ground, black pepper
vodka (optional)

Slice the strawberries thinly or halve them using a serrated bread knife. Dust them lightly with the coarsely ground, black pepper and serve.

For a more adventurous touch, arrange the sliced strawberries in an overlapping pattern on a plate, drizzle a little vodka carefully over them and then dust with pepper.

CREME FRAICHE

1 litre whipping cream
4 tsp buttermilk
1 large glass jar or jug

Scald the cream and remove immediately from the heat when you see the first bubble. Stir in the buttermilk (stir it well) and pour into a jug. Cover loosely and leave at room temperature, not in a fridge, for at least 12 hours and up to 24 hours. Don't touch, poke or stir it for all this time. It should have thickened considerably and developed a richer flavour. The crème fraîche will now keep in the fridge for 10 to 14 days.

a best beloved) — there is not much to do with strawberries that is not superfluous to their true nature.

Some of the local newspapers will encourage you to dilute them with rhubarb, and there are recipes for freezing them on trays, then putting them in freezer bags, an admirable way of preserving their looks but a sad disappointment when in mid-winter they come to your tongue, defrosted and mushy, without their essential soul. You just can't freeze a summer's day.

But there are a few exciting and simple things to do with strawberries which are not common knowledge. Strawberries and pepper, for example. Pepper, when it was first imported from Malabar, was so expensive and so efficiently marketed by the Venetians that it was tried on everything. Pepper water, a sort of tea made by boiling peppercorns in water and adding a little sugar, was a cure for the fainting fits of ladies of quality, and also used as a tonic for what was then known as weak blood. Pepper had its day as a topping for hot chocolate, and the present day pepper grinder, while it has undoubted merit as a provider of freshly crushed, still fragrant pepper, was originally invented as an item of conspicuous consumption — people had to see you putting the pepper on and not risk the danger of having it pass un-noticed as a hidden ingredient in a dish. Besides, the pepper was so valuable that it just didn't do to leave it in the kitchen for the cooks to steal, and when dinner was over the pepper mill went back into the locked closet, with the key round the housekeeper's neck.

Since then, pepper has deteriorated into a familiar and therefore ordinary spice, usually referred to in recipes as "P and S to taste." But there are palates in the world which remember some interesting things which pepper goes with, including strawberries. Sliced thin, or halved (a serrated bread knife is the most efficient tool for this), and dusted lightly with fresh ground pepper, the fresh strawberry develops a big round flavour, with its natural sweetness highlighted by the slight bite of the pepper.

But pepper also goes extremely well with vodka. (Very, very cold vodka, in a very, very cold shot glass, the top sprinkled fairly generously with black pepper or not quite so generously with cayenne, and "Prosit," down it goes, Russian style. Just don't burp near an open flame . . .) And so, if you want to be a little adventurous, arrange the sliced strawberries in a slightly overlapping pattern on your most handsome white plate, drizzle a little vodka carefully over them, and then the pepper, fairly coarsely ground and preferably black, so that you can see it.

Strawberry season is also a great time to perfect the art of making *creme fraiche*, mainly because *creme fraiche*, which so many cookbooks insist upon as essential, really needs a litre of whipping cream to turn out properly, and without something like fresh strawberries as an excuse for overindulgence it often sits in the fridge and rots, causing you to swear never to use it again.

While the need for *creme fraiche* is not quite as universal as the gourmets would have us believe, fresh strawberries and, a little later on, local strawberries, go with it in unforgettable combination. Try it, use it on the berries, and stir a couple of tablespoons of it into the pan juices next time you fry a chicken.

Learning to use unfamiliar ingredients is always easier when they just happen to be lying around, and don't have to be specially made. So, as soon as the first local berries come on the market, make a litre of *creme fraiche*.

Scald a litre of whipping cream, which means putting it in a heavy saucepan and heating it just until the first bubbles appear — about 95 degrees if you want to be technical, but the first bubble usually works as an indicator. Take it immediately off the heat, stir in 4 teaspoons buttermilk (stir it well) and pour it into the jug. Cover it loosely, and leave it at comfortable room temperature, not in the fridge and not in the sun, probably at the back of the kitchen counter. Don't touch it, jiggle it, poke it or stir it for at least 12 hours, by which time it should have thickened considerably, and developed a flavour much richer than the cream you started with. I usually leave mine for close to 18 to 24 hours, but time is not critical. The *creme fraiche* will now keep in the fridge for 10 to 14 days, getting thicker and richer each day. Use lots of it; it is a luxury which, like the strawberries, won't last forever.

And to be completely local, there is fresh spinach, a little muddier than the California or Mexican spinach, but greener, juicier in the leaf and firm — the kind of spinach whose handshake you would instinctively trust.

Take it home, wash it well but quickly, dry the leaves in a salad spinner or with a tea towel (I put them in a clean towel, grab the four corners, take it out the back door and spin it round my head. The neighbours think I'm mad but the kids love it) and make a spinach and strawberry salad. Use one bunch of spinach and half a box of strawberries. Slice the strawberries, make a vinaigrette: Shake 2 parts oil (peanut's best) in a jar with one part lemon juice, a little salt and twice as much pepper (remember the pepper's good with strawberries). Toss the spinach with the berries, and the minute before you eat add the vinaigrette — if you leave spinach sitting dressed it goes soggy. A little fried and crumbled bacon is an interesting addition and makes the salad big enough for a lunch dish, and a tablespoon of the *creme fraiche* shaken in the vinaigrette gives you a very smooth dressing.

SPINACH AND STRAWBERRY SALAD

1 bunch spinach
1/2 box strawberries
peanut oil
lemon juice
salt and pepper

Shake two parts oil with one part lemon juice, a little salt and twice as much pepper. Toss the spinach with the strawberries and just before eating add the vinaigrette. Serve with perhaps some fried and crumbled bacon sprinkled on top or add a tablespoon of crème fraîche to the vinaigrette, shake well and you have a very smooth dressing.

Primitive Pleasures

Sometimes the recipe calls for a low-tech process.

Somebody is always making something at an international folk festival. Quilts and wood carvings, string toys, dancing dolls from Quebec, decorated eggs from the Ukraine, and music from all over the world. But the place that gets the most constant crowds is a very basic kitchen built around an old-style beehive-shaped wood-burning brick oven.

Doukhobor women in headscarves work alongside a group of mad haggis makers. A skinny-hipped Italian hurls pizza fifteen feet in the air and a Northern Chinese family makes noodles completely by hand, stretching them like a skipping rope — they start off with flour and water and five minutes later they each have an armful of noodles ready to go into the pot. Everything that is made goes into some kind of pot, or it goes into the oven — bread, chicken, salmon, bannock, scones, lamb, tourtieres — and there is never a lack of audience watching it go in and come out.

But this is not *haute cuisine* they are watching. No *chefs* — just cooks. Some of the groups bring pre-prepared super-dishes — loaves of plaited bread and the occasional elaborate cake, but that's usually the first time they do it. Almost everything thereafter is made on site, out of flour and potatoes and cheap meat and fish that usually is not salmon. It's pleasant cooking, most of it based on recipes only recently translated into writing, because the originals were just told: "A little of this and a bit more of that, then you mix it like this . . ." Peasant cooking, grandma cooking, farm cooking — no microwaves, no thermostats, no copper pans and no fancy photographs to measure up to.

The 'Ksan from Hazelton make bannock. They take a bowl of flour, add lard and salt and water and baking powder — there isn't really a recipe — and throw it into a black old skillet over an open fire. Some of it they make into balls the size of a walnut. Then they take a stick, a long round stick with the bark peeled off, and mould this lump around the end of it (imagine a plaster cast around your finger).

The first time they did this it was for children. Half a dozen kids each with a stick turned the ends around over the fire. When it was done (some of it brown, some of it black, and some of it, but not much of it, just right), they slid the little sleeves of bannock off the stick and filled them with jam. Six smiling kids.

Two hours later, everybody was a kid. Sixty-year-old women, super-cool, green-haired teenagers, tourists from France, all of them with a little bit of dough on the end of a stick and a smile on the end of their faces. They wanted to eat something primitive, and they wanted to be part of a basic, uncomplicated, low-tech process.

I took some of the dough and rolled it into a foot-long skinny snake, a little thinner than my little finger. We spiralled it round the end of the stick and cooked it slowly over the fire. We could have stayed there all day and all night — everybody wanted to play, and have a part of something that didn't come out of a packet. It was a party — no booze, no invitations, just a spontaneous eruption of a good time.

Next morning we took the same ingredients (some flour, some salt, some baking powder and some fat) and gave them to twenty small children. We added some sugar, and some sultanas and an egg, and suddenly it wasn't bannock, it was muffins, or it was teacakes, or hot biscuits — everybody had a different name for it. Some of it went into muffin tins, some into frypans, some onto cookie sheets. Some of it was wet and sloppy, some of it was dry and stiff — each child had made her or his own highly personal version. Some of it looked like rock cakes and some like pancakes. Some children had lots of flour on their faces, and some even more.

Some forgot the sugar, some didn't want egg, and some put cheese in instead of sultanas. One put in cheese and grated coconut and yogurt as well as the sultanas, and used apple juice instead of water. But fifteen minutes later, when they were all cooked, they had one thing in common. Each and every one of them had the best thing they had ever tasted. It was hot, and fresh, and different; it was messy and it was improvised; it didn't have a name or a price tag on it, and there was no one word to describe it, except the kind of big smile that lasts all day.

The most important ingredients of primitive cooking are the freedom to make mistakes and the courage to accept and appreciate them. Cooking is an art, not a paint-by-numbers kit in which we just fill in the blank spaces. So let me give you a few non-recipes, each of which will give you, your friends and your family a lot of pleasure.

First of all, bannock. About 2 cups of flour, and 3 or 4 tablespoons of oil or butter or lard. A teaspoonful of baking powder, 2 or 3 good pinches of salt and enough water, milk, beer or apple juice to make it into a stiffish dough. Pat it out about half an inch thick, and fry it, bake it (in a medium-hot oven) or throw it on a barbecue that's not too hot. That's real bannock, good campfire bread which you can cook on a picnic, wrap around sticks, or serve with a good fish stew. Add

BANNOCK

2 cups flour
3 - 4 tbsp oil, butter or lard
1 tsp baking powder
2 - 3 good pinches of salt
water, milk, beer or apple juice to make a stiffish dough

Mix all ingredients together, pat it out about half an inch thick, then fry it, bake it (in medium/hot oven) or throw it on a barbecue that isn't too hot.

SCONES

Add a little sugar and some sultanas to the bannock.

CHEESE BISCUITS

Add some cheese to the bannock.

BREAKFAST BISCUITS

Make as for Bannock but substitute sour cream for some of the liquid. Spread with butter when hot and serve.

TORTILLA ESPAÑOLA OR SPANISH OMELETTE

2 unpeeled potatoes, diced small
1 onion, chopped
olive oil
6 - 8 eggs
2 good pinches of salt
cayenne pepper

Fry the potatoes in the oil until half cooked. Add the chopped onion and fry well. Beat the eggs with the salt and cayenne pepper and pour over the potatoes and onions. Cook until bottom is crusty, put a plate over the pan and turn it over. Cook the bottom until that is crusty too. Eat hot or cold. It can be baked in the oven instead of frying.

LAZY MAN'S CHICKEN OR DRUNKEN CHICKEN

1 chicken
1 carrot, chopped
1 onion, quartered
1 bay leaf
4 tbsp soya sauce
2 tbsp sugar
juice of a lemon
2 oz whiskey
cayenne pepper

Boil enough water to cover the chicken in a pan with the carrot, onion and bay leaf. Put half a dozen knives, forks or spoons inside the chicken (they conduct the heat) and place it in the pan. Bring back to the boil and cook for 5 minutes. Turn off the heat, put the lid on and leave until it's cold, which will be most of the day. Remove chicken and garnish.

Make the sauce by mixing the soya sauce, sugar, lemon juice and whiskey, sprinkle with the cayenne pepper and dip each piece of chicken in it as you eat.

a little bit of sugar and some sultanas and it's a scone, add some cheese and it's cheese biscuits, substitute sour cream for some of the liquid and it's hot biscuits for breakfast, spread it copiously with butter and you'll fight with your friends for the last piece.

Then tortilla Espanole, which is a Spanish omelette. Cut a couple of potatoes into small dice, leaving the skins on. Fry them in some olive oil until they're half cooked. Add a chopped onion (some are big, some are small) and fry until it smells nice. Beat up half a dozen (that's five, six or eight) eggs with a couple of large pinches of salt and some hot red cayenne pepper and pour them over the potatoes and onions. Cook until the bottom is crusty, put a plate over the pan and turn it over. Cook the bottom (which was once the top) until it's crusty too. Eat it hot or cold; it's never the same twice running but it's always delicious. And if you don't want to fry it you can bake it in the oven.

Finally, for the ultimate in effortless cooking, Lazy Man's Chicken, which the Chinese call white cooked chicken, or drunken chicken. Put a chicken in a pot just big enough for it, and cover it with cold water. Take the chicken out, bring the water to the boil with a carrot (cut up), an onion (quartered) and a bay leaf. Put half a dozen knives, forks or spoons inside the chicken (they conduct the heat) and put the chicken back in the pot. Bring it back to the boil, and cook five minutes. Turn off the heat, put the lid on, and leave it until it's cold, which takes most of the day, thereby making this a great Saturday dish because you can go out. Take out the chicken, arrange a few tomatoes or sprigs of parsley around it — whatever you have at hand — and make the sauce: four tablespoons of soya sauce, two tablespoons of sugar, juice of a lemon and a couple of ounces of whiskey. Sprinkle with hot cayenne pepper, mix well, and dip each piece of chicken in it as you eat. A truly wonderful summer dish with virtually no effort.

Behind Closed Doors

Tucked away in every kitchen are
those things that are too nice to use.

My mother has a closet full of things that are "too nice to use." She
has Belgian lace handkerchiefs and leather gloves, soft as butter, from
Spain. She has small bottles of perfume and large bottles of perfume,
she has shoes, really expensive shoes, bought in Italy and never worn,
black silk slips and petticoats still in their boxes and the original tissue
paper, and she has a bunch of cashmere sweaters, used only by the
moths which brave the mothballs to indulge themselves with
absolutely no concern for tomorrow.

Most people's kitchens are like my mother's closet, filled with
expensive, rich and flavourful things bought on a whim — things like
extra-virgin olive oil, a little sack of Madagascar pepper, a jar of beluga
caviar, a pretty little carved oak spice rack with the checked cotton
tops still tied with ribbon, a pot of pesto, half used, the rest white with
mold. They sit there, day by day, scaring us with their niceness, with
their expensive status, silently telling us that we are not good enough
for them, not today. Tomorrow, if somebody nice comes to supper
and if we have time to find a recipe that is nice enough to use these
things in, and if we can convince ourselves that we can make the recipe
properly. So we finish up making the same thing we made the last time
they came, while the nice-things continue to sit in the fridge, victims
of their own luxury and our own fear of trying.

Take that extra-virgin olive oil, bought because a magazine article
said that Jackie Onassis uses a few drops of it in her salads. It's about
as expensive as Chanel Number Five, so you flick a few drops on
lettuce and nobody leaps three feet in the air, nobody really seems
to notice, let alone get ecstatic. But find a lettuce fresh from the
garden, shake off the dew, and then be generous, plain downright
wasteful, with the extra-virgin. Then sprinkle a few drops of juice
squeezed from the plumpest, shiniest and freshest lemon you can find
in the store, a pinch or two of salt rubbed between your fingers, and
a little fresh pepper — *then* you will have an unforgettable salad,
flavoured not only with the oil, but with generosity, which translates
into: "What the heck, we only live once."

"Waste," somebody is sure to say, "so expensive." But you're not

ORANGE SALAD

2 medium oranges, firm and
shiny-skinned
1 medium onion
olive oil
ground black pepper

*Peel the oranges and
remove all the white pith.
With a very sharp knife cut
the orange crosswise into
slices as thick as a
telephone cord. Slice the
onion crosswise into the
thinnest slices you can
manage.*

*Separate the rings and lay
two or three of them on each
slice of orange. Arrange the
whole lot, slightly
overlapping but in one layer,
on a plate, sprinkle well with
the ground black pepper
and pour a generous amount
of olive oil over the whole
thing.*

*Allow it to sit for about half
an hour before serving as
either a combination salad
or dessert or as an
appetizer.*

wasting it, it's going into your stomach, the most important part of your anatomy, past your tastebuds, over your tongue and five minutes after that you'll still be sucking flavours from between your teeth. Now that you have the habit of using it, of not being afraid of it, try some experimental things, like orange salad. Very easy, just peel a couple of medium-sized, firm, shiny-skinned oranges. Take all the white pith off, and with a very sharp knife cut the orange crosswise into slices as thick as a telephone cord. Slice a medium onion crosswise into the thinnest slices you can manage, separate the rings and lay two or three of them on each slice of orange. Arrange the whole lot, slightly overlapping but in one layer, on a plate, sprinkle it all well with ground black pepper, and pour over the whole thing a healthy generosity of olive oil. Let it sit for half a hour (even two hours won't hurt it) and serve it either after your dinner, as a combination salad or dessert, or as an appetizer. Whatever oil and juice is left on the plate you either eat sopped up with bread or pour into a little jar to use as dressing next time you make a salad, to give a brand new identity to a broiled chicken breast, or even to dress up some stir-fried vegetables. Useful, different and surprisingly pleasant, this orange/onion/olive oil mixture is a variation on a Persian salad.

Now pesto. You either make it yourself from a garden full of fresh basil, or you buy it pre-made in a little pot for almost as much per pound as you'd pay for a Porche. First of all, if you grow your own, make lots and freeze it. But don't put the cheese in until you defrost it — the cheese flavour will then come through much more pungently (which also means that you use less).

And if you're buying it, then it's time you stopped. A cheap blender will pay for itself in a month if you make your own pesto, and a food processor (you don't need anything fancy) in six. In Italy, pesto is sort of summer peanut butter; there's always some hanging around when the basil is growing, and you can find all sorts of uses for it — not only on pasta, but on chicken or pork chops, on eggs both fried and hardboiled, thinned out with a little white wine as a salad dressing, even added to mayonnaise, with a tomato chopped fine, two cloves of garlic and a couple of anchovy fillets, whizzed together and used to transform plain old boiled potatoes.

Basil, however, doesn't grow in the winter, pine nuts are expensive, and so is parmesan cheese.

But almost every supermarket and assuredly every Chinese corner store now sells Chinese parsley, year round, for a fraction of the price of basil. And any cheese store which sells ungrated parmesan will also sell asiago, again considerably cheaper. Asiago has much of the flavour of parmesan, not quite the pungency, and is a wonderful cheese in that fresh it is cuttable, like cheddar, and tastes wonderful but mild with apples or black olives. As it gets old and dry and hard (the fate of all cheese in these days of the self-defrosting refrigerator), it becomes sharper, and bigger in flavour; in fact, an ideal cheese for adding to a pesto sauce.

Wash the Chinese parsley well and cut off the roots just below the leaves. Put it in the blender, or food processor, with 2 cloves of garlic, peeled, 1 cup of good vegetable oil (peanut oil's fine) ½ teaspoon salt, 4 tablespoons chopped walnuts, and whizz it smooth. Then add the fine grated Asiago, and there you have an inexpensive, different pesto. Use it as you would any other pesto, give it to your friends in little jars, put it on pasta or in vegetable soups, and when the Fall comes, use fresh hazelnuts instead of walnuts, or spinach instead of Chinese parsley.

And before we get off the subject of walnuts, walnut oil is hideously expensive. Most French restaurants cheat. They take a litre of safflower oil and add a cop of chopped walnuts to it, let is soak for a couple of weeks, strain it, and *voila!* Walnut oil for salads all winter long. Walnuts are at their cheapest and best when they are absolutely fresh in the fall, and they will stay fresh if you keep them tightly sealed in the freezer.

The walnut oil you can put in little bottles, for which you make nice little labels (that's why offices have copiers), and give to your friends. They won't use it because everybody knows how expensive walnut oil is.

ORIENTAL PESTO

1 bunch Chinese parsley (also called cilantro or fresh coriander)
2 cloves garlic, peeled
1 cup good vegetable oil (cold pressed safflower or peanut oil)
1/2 tsp salt
4 tbsp fine chopped walnuts
1/2 cup grated asiago cheese

Wash the Chinese parsley well and cut off stems one inch from the root. Put everything else, except the cheese, in the blender or processor and whiz it smooth. Add the cheese. Serve as you would traditional pesto. Can be frozen without the cheese. Hazelnuts can be substituted for walnuts.

WALNUT OIL

1 litre safflower oil
1 cup chopped walnuts

Allow the walnuts to soak in the oil for a couple of weeks, then strain it and bottle it. The best walnuts are the fresh ones in the fall which can be kept tightly sealed in the freezer.

Mutiny On The Bounty

What to do
when your garden explodes.

The sun shines, the rain falls, and God, because She likes flowers, makes the gardens grow. We get tans, the tomatoes get ripe, and suddenly, like those unfortunates with kittens to give away, for a whole month we have no friends. People don't call back, because their answering machines mustn't be working, because they had your number but lost it, or because the children had to be quarantined ("nothing serious but we just didn't think we should run the risk of spreading it").

They all have reasons, they all have to be careful, because if they're not, then just as they're about to sneak up to your door with a box of ripe tomatoes, three over-sized zucchini and a large paper bag of green beans, they're likely to find you arriving at *their* door with almost exactly the same thing.

Harvest time is not a time of moderation. Those exhuberant seeds we planted in the hopeful days of springtime, those extra rows of peas, the beets, the beans, the tomatoes and zucchini, they struggle through May, make a few leaves in July and suddenly, totally promiscuous, in the late days of summer they have fruit, all of them, all at once. Everything is ripe and ready; it has to be canned, dried, frozen, eaten, given away or left to rot.

Everybody has recipes for pickles, for zucchini bread, for tomato chowchow, for relishes and little pots of stuff to tie ribbons 'round and give away at Christmas, while the newspapers are full of even more helpful hints, like how to build a ski cabin out of freeze-dried zucchini or how to knit a spring sweater with runner beans. But nobody says to you that the finest tomato in the world is the one growing in a sunny corner of your garden at 11 AM one gorgeous September morning, the one you pick, nick slightly with your teeth, and then dip into salt in the palm of your hand before you eat it, still warm, dripping with juice and tasting like no other tomato ever has before or will again.

The Japanese do this with strawberries — I've seen single strawberry plants sitting in pots outside Tokyo houses, and every morning before papa-san went to work he would water and prune and dust his plant, feed it and fuss over it, and if there were five people in the family then there would be five strawberries only allowed to grow. On the big day, the day of total and absolute perfection of ripeness, the father would take the day off. The whole family, dressed in their best, would make the day a personal and private festival, a celebration, and after tea and appropriate compliments, after the admiration of the plant, of the berries, of father's skill, the individual strawberries would be snipped off, further admired, and then, in careful concentration, eaten. Each drop of juice touched each tastebud, and even in the middle of the industrial jungle, the work- and consumer-oriented society that is today's Japan, people still remember the primal nature of food that they helped to grow.

Restaurants are learning this today — there are not many places still serving those "garden fresh vegetables" which come defrosted from the packet to your plate, pausing briefly for the microwave. Fresh salads, local vegetables, even edible chrysanthemums — we're beginning to realize that all good things don't have to start in California. In fact, a lot of our good things are going to California. And to France, to Germany, to Japan, to the fancy hotels of England.

In New York's Grand Central Station Oyster Bar, the North American Mecca for oyster eaters, our golden mantle oysters fetch a higher price than the famous bluepoints. In France they eat our *Chanterelles,* flown daily, in season, from Kelowna to Paris. Pacific smoked salmon, cheddar from the Fraser Valley, cranberries and beef — they're all exported while in Hong Kong the most popular brand of a special Chinese sausage (*laup cheung*) is made in Vancouver and air-freighted weekly.

But all of these people also eat their own delicacies. We waste food in North America because of our prejudices. A recent two-year study of Philadelphia's garbage showed that 31 percent of the food purchased in that city ended up in the trash can, and questionnaires addressed to a representative cross-section showed that nearly 25 percent of the rejected food was in the garbage because "nobody wanted to try it." I'm not suggesting that we all start to eat chocolate-covered ants, or the other fad foods that from time to time become so popular, and I'm certainly not attempting to resurrect my grandmother, who made me eat my mutton fat before I could have rice pudding. But it would be nice if we got to be a little more adventurous, and let a few local things become routine in our daily dinners.

Next time you fry chicken, nothing fancy, just your normal way of frying chicken, throw a big handful of blueberries into the pan two minutes before you're ready to serve. Stir them around with the chicken, sprinkle a little lemon juice over the top, a little extra pepper, and *presto* — something local, something different, but not something with a fancy name, just "that chicken you made last time, remember,

CHICKEN AND BLUEBERRIES

1 cut up chicken
a large handful of blueberries
a little lemon juice
freshly ground pepper

Fry chicken in some butter. Two minutes before serving throw in large handful of blueberries. Stir with the chicken, sprinkle a little lemon juice over the top and some freshly ground pepper and serve. (NO blueberries, substitute peaches).

FRIED TOMATOES 1

2 large green tomatoes
flour
salt and pepper
oregano

Slice the tomatoes thickly and dip them in the flour with a little salt, pepper and oregano mixed in. Coat both sides well. Fry over medium heat in a little bacon fat until brown on both sides. Eat with fried eggs.

FRIED TOMATOES 2

2 large green tomatoes
flour
few tsp brown sugar

Slice or halve the tomatoes. Dip the cut sides in flour and fry gently over low/medium heat in a little butter. Turn them when the underside is a light brown and sprinkle a few teaspoons of brown sugar over them. Cook again until the underside is brown, turn again and cook until the sugar caramelizes. Serve them caramel side up with turkey, chicken or pork roast.

ZUCCHINI LATKES

2 cups coarsely grated
zucchini
1/2 medium onion, grated
1/2 cup flour
1 tsp baking powder
1 egg, well beaten, or
1/4 cup beer mixed with 1
tbsp oil
1/2 tsp each, salt and
pepper
1/2 tsp tarragon
1 lemon, quartered

*Mix the zucchini with the
onion. Mix the flour with the
baking powder, salt and
tarragon. Sprinkle the
zucchini with the flour and
mix well. Add the egg or
beer/oil and mix again. Heat
a pan over medium/high
heat, add a little oil and fry
the mixture in small cakes
(about a tablespoon at a
time) until they are light to
medium brown. Eat them
with bacon, applesauce and
sour cream, or a roast
chicken.*

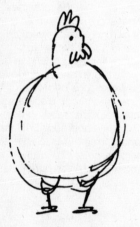

the one with the blueberries . . ."

Pretty soon you'll be grating a little fresh ginger into the pan when you start the chicken, knowing full well that it will taste good with the blueberries, and a bit later on you'll be slicing up local peaches to put in because you haven't got blueberries. Once you get used to local things your kitchen becomes a different place. Fifteen years ago we wouldn't eat mushrooms . . .

Now those tomatoes. Take a couple of the green ones (the good big ones), hard and just too late to ripen. Slice them thickish, and dip them in flour with a little salt, pepper and oregano mixed in. Make sure both sides are well coated. Then fry them in the fat left in the pan after you've cooked a couple of slices of bacon. Just brown both sides over medium heat, and eat them with fried eggs. Thick slices of apple (just cut them straight across and eat around the seeds) are also wonderful fried in bacon fat and then dusted with a little cinnamon.

Next time you have a turkey, or a chicken, or best of all a pork roast, take a couple more green tomatoes, slice them if they're big, halve them if they're medium, dip the cut sides in flour and fry, gently (low/medium), in a little butter. Turn them when the underside is a nice light brown, and sprinkle a few teaspoons of brown sugar over them. Cook again until the underside is brown, then turn again and cook until the sugar caramelizes. Serve them with the caramel side up — a very different, semi-sweet, semi-sour flavour which has to be very local, because not everyplace has green tomatoes.

And if you want something utterly gorgeous, something not just too good for company, but so good that you'll always have difficulty in getting enough of it to the table to fill a serving plate, try Zucchini Latkes.

Mix the 2 cups grated zucchini with ½ a medium onion. Mix ½ cup flour and 1 teaspoon each baking powder, salt and tarragon. Sprinkle the zucchini with the flour and mix well. Add one egg or ¼ cup beer/1 tablespoon oil and mix again. Heat a pan (medium/high), add a little oil and fry the mixture in little cakes (about a tablespoon at a time) until they are light to medium brown. Eat them with bacon, or with applesauce and sour cream, or a roast chicken. I have friends who spread jam on them at breakfast, and on one glorious Sunday of self-indulgence we ate them with caviar.

Next time you see your friends coming up the walk, get out the grater. Don't let the mix sit around, or it gets soggy — just make it, cook it and eat it.

The Forgotten Art Of Generous Cooking

Between Thanksgiving and Christmas the papers and the magazines are filled with complicated recipes for terribly expensive desserts, frightfully sophisticated party snacks and unusual punches, sometimes called wassail bowls, with everything so desperately original that the shopping alone will take a week of eight-hour days, and the preparation almost another.

All of this fuss is based on the myth that the Canadian winter is a six-month bacchanal, a continuous, carefree and self-indulgent festival of overeating and overspending, with our houses open 24 hours a day to guests, both invited and uninvited, none of whom can be offered such simple things as bread and cheese or a fried egg sandwich.

Occasionally there are recipes for leftovers, but they too are a little exotic — cold roast beef with caviar and quail eggs, or soufflé of salmon and pheasant breast, while the problem facing most of us is what to do with the remains of a twice re-heated, obviously unpopular meat loaf which even the next-door cat — the hungry, sleep-in-one-house, eat-in-another, next-door cat — refuses to touch.

But we don't get many of those old-fashioned grandmotherly recipes, those comforting, cold day, utterly simple things we remember not just with our taste buds but with our emotions. The old-fashioned recipes — three parts of improvisation and one part generosity, stirred well with love and cooked until you feel better.

Perhaps it's because generosity is so hard to find in today's kitchens. The comforting art has become a terrifying science. What used to be a bit of this and bit of that has gone metric, and it also insists upon imported *this* and Canada Grade A *that*. We worry that it won't look right or taste right if we don't follow the recipe exactly, we get scared of putting in too much of anything and end up putting in too little. Which explains why so many dishes that sound so good end up tasting dull.

Leftovers are the best way there is to learn the simplicities of generous cooking. Cooking leftovers is an art practised over the world. The Scots (or is it the Scottish?) bludgeoned us into an appreciation of haggis, which essentially is the Scottish butcher's answer to his

BREAD AND BUTTER PUDDING

6 - 8 slices of stale bread
2 eggs
2 cups milk
3 tbsp brown sugar
sultanas

Butter the bread slices generously and cover the bottom of a frypan or casserole (about 8" across) with a single layer of them, buttered side down. Sprinkle generously with sultanas. Cover, buttered side down, with another layer of bread. Beat the eggs with the milk and sugar and pour over the bread. Make sure everything is well soaked. Sprinkle a little more sugar on top and put in the oven at 350°F for half an hour. Add a little brandy or sherry to the eggs for variation or some grated lemon zest in with the sultanas or use fresh blueberries, raspberries or blackberries instead of sultanas and cream instead of milk.

otherwise unsaleable leftovers of sheep. The Irish dealt with an excess of cold boiled potatoes by turning them into potato bread and scones. The native people hung fish on lines to dry and the Japanese did much the same thing with seaweed. Ordinary, simple, non-professional people cooked simple food with simple techniques and simple equipment — none of it using expensive ingredients, but all of it made with enthusiasm, generosity and little bits of this and that.

One of my big successes with leftovers is stale bread pudding, a vague memory of childhood in my grandmother's boarding house. It is ridiculously simple, a quick and easy dessert which children not only love but can easily make. Tarted up a little, with whipped cream or a little booze, it's good enough for very sophisticated company, and cold, cut into chunks, it's an interesting addition to a lunchbox.

Generously butter 6 or 8 slices of stale bread. Cover the bottom of a frypan (or a casserole, something fireproof and about 8 inches across) with a single layer of bread slices, buttered side down. Sprinkle generously with sultanas and cover, buttered side down, with another layer of the bread. Beat 2 eggs with 2 cups of milk and 3 tablespoons of sugar, pour it over the bread and squeeze it up and down a bit until everything is soaked. Sprinkle a bit more sugar on top and put it in the oven at 350°F for half an hour while you eat dinner. I like to put a little brandy or sherry in with the eggs, I prefer brown sugar to white and sometimes I mix a little grated lemon zest in with the sultanas. Sometimes I use fresh blueberries instead of sultanas, sometimes frozen raspberries or fresh blackberries, and sometimes cream instead of milk. In a pinch even canned milk works.

Whatever you use, the top goes brown and crispy, the inside is fruity and squishy, and you may find you prefer it cooked a bit longer for a crispier top. Whatever you do, this pudding is foolproof. If you're terribly insecure you can tart it up with whipped cream, or custard, even make a rum sauce, but none of this artifice is really necessary — the pudding stands alone in its simple generosity.

Let's talk about generosity some more. Cooking has always been an art of economy. Grandmas learned how to save pennies because they had to. Grandmas were raised in a world where nobody had very much: "All we had to play with on the Prairies was corncobs." But Grandmas' food always tasted wonderful, even if they didn't have access to racks of imported spices. "Waste not, want not" was a basic principle of survival which not only made small children finish their dinners but also spawned the whole food-preserving industry. This made a fortune for old Mr. Schneider and the Jolly Green Giant, but made *us* lazy. What we once would have made we bought and we got used to bland, inoffensive, ungenerous flavours.

We forgot how to put ourselves into our dinner and we forgot how to make do. We bought stuff that would keep forever, and we subconsciously learned false economy that had nothing to do with money. We forgot that Grandma's dinners tasted better because she always put in an extra pinch of something.

Try this shepherd's pie as a simple test of generosity as a spice. It's cheap and simple. It was once made of leftover lamb, the Sunday roast ground up, but it's extremely good with ground beef, provided that you don't buy the fattiest and cheapest you can find. Buy a bit less but buy a bit better. And be generous with everything else except salt.

Boil and mash half a dozen medium-sized potatoes (or three big ones, halved). Mash them with a generous amount of pepper and about 4 ounces of butter. Set aside. Slice and chop 3 medium onions, then fry them transparent in a little oil, and stir in 1½ pounds of good ground beef. Stir it about a lot until it separates. Grate a big carrot into the pan, and add 1½ teaspoons of rosemary, 1 teaspoon salt and 2 teaspoons Worchestershire sauce. Stir it a lot more.

Put the meat and onions in a casserole or baking dish. Pat it down. Put the potatoes on top, and pat them down with a fork, which will make a nice pattern on top. Mound it up to the middle. Dot the top with butter, or brush it with an egg yolk. Bake in a 400°F oven until the top is browned, and eat it immediately with peas. Don't hide the big generous smile on your face.

SHEPHERD'S PIE

6 medium potatoes (or 3 large)
4 oz butter
3 medium onions, chopped
1 1/2 lb good ground beef
oil
1 large carrot
1 1/2 tsp rosemary
1 tsp salt
2 tsp Worcestershire sauce
pepper

Boil and mash the potatoes with a generous amount of pepper and the butter. Set aside. Fry the chopped onions in a little oil until transparent and add the ground beef. Stir until it separates. Grate the carrot into the pan and add rosemary, salt and Worcestershire sauce. Stir well.

Put the meat and onions in a casserole or baking dish and pat it down. Pile the potatoes on top and pat them down with a fork making a nice pattern on the top and mounding it up to the middle. Dot the top with butter, or brush with an egg yolk. Bake in the oven at 400°F until nicely browned. Serve with green peas.

Taking Control Of The Festive Season

When visions of mayhem dance through your head, it's time to make life simpler.

CHICKEN LIVER PATÉ

1 lb chicken livers
1 medium onion
5 oz butter
2 anchovy fillets
1/2 tsp ground pepper
cayenne pepper
1 oz brandy, rye, scotch or sherry

Melt 3 oz butter in a frypan over medium heat. Add the chicken livers and chopped onion. Cook until the livers are just done (pink inside), add the anchovy fillets and ground pepper. Stir well until the anchovies have melted then scrape everything into a blender or food processor. Add 2 oz of butter, the cayenne pepper and either brandy, rye, scotch or sherry. Whiz it smooth and put into a bowl, or small bowls, whilst warm. Smooth the top, put a little melted butter on top and allow to cool.

T'was the month before Christmas and all through the house the cooks were all stirring with many a grouse.
The ingredients so costly, most of them rare, all the cooks needing to drive here and there,
to pick up the ginger and two pounds of suet.
Three saucepans, four bowls — how did Grandmother do it?
And after five hours of stirring and mixing, the dishwasher's full and it suddenly needs fixing.
The kitchen's a mess, the tempers are frayed, the kids won't clean up unless they get paid.
And all of a sudden a terrible clatter — the cat has jumped in and then out of the batter!
A man on the phone wants to sell you some shares, the dog's in the garbage and from the upstairs the noise you can hear is the bath overflowing, while the stain in the ceiling is steadily growing.
Then the phone rings again: "Merry Christmas to you. Miss Smith here at Visa; your account's overdue."

It doesn't have to be such a panic. There are simple things, nice things, and easy things, all quick to make, and the time you save can be your private Christmas present to yourself.

Sometimes a party just isn't a party without a dip, and the simplest and quickest dip of all is 2 tablespoons of peanut butter mashed up with the juice of a lemon and two crushed cloves of garlic. Bung it in the blender or mash it well with a fork (it will get stiffer than when it started), then dilute it with an equal amount of plain yogurt. Cut up a few vegetables (carrots, mushrooms, cauliflower, green peppers, broccoli — whatever's in the fridge, even rutabaga) and if you're really fast you can have it on the table before they've finished apologizing ("We should have called first but we thought we'd just drop in . . .")

The simplest of all chicken liver pâtés (the fancy books will call it a mousse and demand cream, egg whites, a Gucci apron and a full set of brand new copper pots) can be made in fifteen minutes, will take two hours to set and develop flavour, and will keep for two weeks in the refrigerator. If you make a bit extra, buy a couple of nice pots, fill them with the pâté and wrap them in cellophane. Then you have the neighbours' present taken care of. I buy teacups in the Sally Ann for just this purpose.

Melt three ounces of butter in a frypan over medium heat. Add one pound of chicken livers (fresh are better than frozen) and a medium onion. Cook about five minutes until the livers are just done (pink inside), add two anchovy fillets and about half a teaspoon of ground pepper. Stir well until the anchovies melt, then scrape everything from the pan into the blender or food processor. Add another two ounces of butter, a good pinch of cayenne pepper and an ounce of brandy, rye, scotch or sherry. Whizz it all smooth, and scrape it out into small bowls or cups while it's still warm. Smooth the top, put a little more melted butter over it (to keep it from going brown in the fridge) and let it cool.

Serve it hot in a bowl, surrounded by crackers or toast. Or, if you're careful, you can dip the bowl in hot water for 30 seconds, invert it over a plate and shake it out, like a mold. Only one pan to wash, and the blender. Just remember not to salt liver pâté until you serve it, then it won't go dark.

Homemade roasted peanuts are another of the really quick and easies — make them once and you'll never buy another can. Heat about a tablespoon of oil in the bottom of a heavy frypan, then add four (at the most six) ounces of raw shelled peanuts (not roasted or salted), with or without the brown skins. Cook over medium heat for about fifteen minutes, stirring constantly to keep them from burning. You can tell when they're done, partly because they start to change colour but mostly because of the warm, round, lovely smell they develop, the smell that peanuts *ought* to have, a smell that is the lovechild of good coffee and fresh popcorn. It moves out of the pan and makes itself at home, first at the kitchen table and then in front of the television. Children will come home without being called for this smell, visitors will look at you with respect and admiration, and you yourself, the purist at work, will try each peanut, one after another, just to see that the peak of perfection is neither accident nor illusion. To be really perfect they must be dusted with salt, and left to cool for ten minutes. They will keep in a screwtop jar, but they never get a chance to. Hazelnuts or almonds are even more wonderful, but they burn quicker, so practice on peanuts first.

The simplest appetizer of all is fresh mushrooms in a mason jar, whole if they're small, quartered if they're big, with 2 tablespoons olive oil, the juice of a lemon, ½ teaspoon salt, ½ teaspoon pepper and 1 teaspoon of green dill, sweet basil or oregano. Shake well (make sure the lid's on) and leave 30 minutes. They won't keep more than an hour or two, and they won't freeze, but I've yet to see any leftovers.

These take just a little longer, but are still an extraordinarily hot party snack. There are eight or nine chicken wings to a pound, and

MARINATED MUSHROOMS

fresh mushrooms (enough to fill a Mason jar)
2 tbsp olive oil
juice of a lemon
1/2 tsp salt
1/2 tsp pepper
1 tsp green dill, sweet basil or oregano

Put the mushrooms, whole if small, quartered if big, into a mason jar. Add olive oil, lemon juice, salt, pepper and dill, basil or oregano. Shake well and leave for 30 minutes.

CHICKEN WINGS - MULTICULTURAL

BASIC RECIPE

chicken wings
cornstarch
4 tbsp oil

Cut each chicken wing through the joints into three pieces. Simmer the tips with a carrot and onion for a future stock or soup. Dust the other two pieces of each wing with cornstarch. Heat the oil in a heavy frypan over medium/high heat, lay in the wings and fry for one minute on each side.

JAPANESE-STYLE

Add 2 tbsp soy sauce and 1 tsp sugar. Stir well and make sure each chicken wing is covered. Cook slowly for ten minutes, dust with a little cayenne pepper and serve.

FRENCH-STYLE

Add 1 tsp thyme, a sprinkle of salt and large sprinkle of pepper. Stir it all well, cook for ten minutes, add a jigger of whipping cream, boil for one minute and serve.

ITALIAN-STYLE

Add 1 tsp oregano, 2 cloves of chopped garlic, half a finely chopped onion, 2 chopped tomatoes and some salt and pepper. Stir it all together, cook for five minutes, add a glass of red wine and cook five minutes more, turning occasionally and serve.

RUTABAGA AND TARRAGON

1 rutabaga
2 tbsp soya sauce
2 tbsp rye whiskey
1 tsp dried (or good handful of fresh) tarragon
1 tsp sugar

Peel and slice the rutabaga into quarter-inch slices, then cut the slices into quarter-inch sticks. Mix the soya sauce, rye whiskey, tarragon and sugar. Toss the rutabaga in this sauce and let it sit for 30 minutes, turning it occasionally. Serve in a shallow bowl.

PEANUT BUTTER DIP

See Page 14 for recipe.

each wing cuts up into two eating pieces and one tip. Simmer the tips with an onion and a carrot for soup (tomorrow's lunch) and dust the other two pieces with cornstarch. Heat 4 tablespoons oil in a heavy frypan, medium-high, lay in the wings with a little space between them and fry one minute on each side. Now you must decide: Japanese, French or Italian.

For Japanese, add two tablespoons soy sauce and one teaspoon sugar. Stir it well and make sure each wing piece gets its share. Cook slowly for ten minutes, dust with a little cayenne pepper and serve immediately, dark brown and sticky, with slices of lemon and lots of paper napkins.

For French, instead of the soy sauce and sugar add a teaspoon of thyme, a sprinkle of salt and a bigger sprinkle of pepper. Turn it all well, cook ten minutes, add a jigger of whipping cream, boil one minute and serve.

For Italian, add a teaspoon of oregano, 2 cloves of chopped garlic, half an onion chopped fine, a couple of cut-up tomatoes and some salt and pepper. Stir it all together, cook five minutes, add half a glass of red wine and cook five minutes more, turning occasionally.

And if you want to surprise yourself, buy a rutabaga for something like 29 cents a pound. Peel it, slice it into ¼-inch sticks. Make a sauce of 2 tablespoons soya sauce, 2 tablespoons rye whiskey and 1 teaspoon dried (or a good handful of fresh) tarragon all mixed with 1 teaspoon of sugar. Toss the rutabaga in the sauce and let it sit for 30 minutes, turning it occasionally. Serve in a shallow bowl. Everybody will eat it, and even stone cold sober nobody will know what it is.

Drastic Measures

Dealing with yesterday's good time.

Leftovers are as hard to get rid of as hangovers. Like the wrong guests at a party, who somehow the morning afterwards, when you hope you'll never see them again, are still there, sitting in the living room looking at you with sad "I gave you the best years of my life" faces. The longer they hang around the more intolerable they become, accusing you of excess, extravagance and overindulgence, accompanied, as background music, by the unforgettable voice of Miss Robinson, Grade 2, who told you the first day she saw you that a bad end awaited you.

Both the face in the mirror and the back end of the turkey leer like horror movies, one from the bathroom and other from the fridge, one promising you a life without a liver and the other an eternity of turkey sandwiches.

Hangovers, like the Rockies, will erode in time and disappear. But leftovers, unless drastic steps are taken, can easily become fixtures, the sort of assets that get listed on the insurance inventory and eventually work their way into your will.

I take drastic steps. Right after dinner I hack the larger pieces of meat off the turkey and put them in the fridge. Everything else on the table — the carcass, dressing, bones, salad, vegetables and odd pickles, unfinished glasses of wine, absolutely *everything* except dessert — I dump into the biggest pot I have. Then I cover the contents with water and let the pot sit until next day. Christmas, Thanksgiving, Easter, turkey, chicken, rabbit, duck or goose, this is the quickest way of simultaneously getting rid of it all and making something useful out of it. Everything in the pot, and cover it with water.

Next morning bring it to the boil and let it simmer four or five hours, or all day if you like. The herbs in the dressing, the spices, the vinegar in the salad, the sweetness of the natural sugars in the brussel sprouts, the soft mushiness of potatoes falling apart, the smoothness that comes from cooked lettuce — they all come together like children's voices in a choir. Nothing sophisticated and obviously nothing predictable, but they are together, and what you are making is the most basic of peasant dishes — back-of-the-stove soup.

MINESTRONE SOUP

2 cups chicken stock (see page 22)
a handful of vegetables, finely chopped
parsley, chopped
1/2 cup small pasta
good pinch of oregano
1 1/2 tsp each salt and pepper

Simmer all the ingredients together for about ten minutes and serve.

HOT AND SOUR SOUP

1 carton chicken stock (see Chapter 6)
some leftover meat
2 mushrooms, sliced
1 onion, chopped
1 tsp ground pepper
1/2 tsp cayenne pepper
1 tbsp vinegar

Simmer all the ingredients, except the vinegar, for ten minutes. Add one tablespoon of vinegar, stir and serve immediately.

CHICKEN LEGS AND RYE

6 chicken legs
1 tbsp oil
1 clove garlic, chopped
1 oz rye
salt and pepper
1 heaped tsp tarragon

Fry the chicken legs in a little oil until just brown on both sides. Sprinkle them with salt, pepper and tarragon. Add the garlic and then pour over the rye, put the lid on and cook for a further 15 minutes.

PORK CHOPS AND RYE

4 pork chops
oil
1 apple, sliced
1 clove garlic, chopped
some rye
salt and pepper
1 heaped tsp thyme

Fry the pork chops in a little oil. Add the salt, pepper, thyme and garlic and fry a few minutes more. Add the apple and a little rye. Cook, with the lid on, stirring occasionally, until the apple has almost melted. Pour in some more rye, bring to the boil and serve immediately.

The first time I lived in France there was nothing but leftovers. Every farmhouse had a big pot, and everything went into it — every last sliver of bone, meat trimmings and tablescraps. While the fire was alight it simmered, and when supper time came it was ladled out into another pot, just enough for how many we were, and some vegetables were added. Whatever vegetables there were — carrots or turnips, onions or wild mushrooms, sometimes nettle leaves and always a big handful of whatever herb grew locally, mostly thyme, which thrives on neglect and covers whole banks by the roadside.

Bread and soup. For a year and a half I ate bread and soup, which is not a complaint. Every night's soup was different and every night's soup was good. Blackbirds, eels, old roosters and ancient ducks — who knew what the soup was supposed to taste like? All these years later I still have the habit of potluck soup, just as I do flipping through a photo album, recalling all the old memories and a few of the recent ones.

When your pot of leftovers has boiled enough and been topped up a few times with more water to keep to bones covered, fish out the larger pieces with a slotted spoon and strain the rest into another pot. This is the moment of pleasure — almost a gallon of rich, multicoloured heavy broth for you to pour into whatever containers you have, old yogurt containers, fancy plastic cliptops or even spare ice cube trays. Let it cool, mark it ("used chicken stock") and freeze it. When the ice cube tray is frozen, shake out the cubes, put them in a plastic bag and put them back in the freezer.

Next time you want to zip up a dreary stew or a thin soup, one or two cubes fished out of the bag will work wonders. Minestrone in a hurry? A carton of the soup brought to the boil, a handful of fine chopped vegetables (anything at all, even potatoes cut into ¼-inch cubes), some chopped parsley, some small pasta (if you have it) and in ten minutes your supper's ready.

Hot and sour soup? This one I do before I freeze it — some lumps of the leftover meat, a couple of sliced mushrooms, a chopped onion, a teaspoon of red cayenne pepper. Let it simmer for ten minutes, add a tablespoon of vinegar, stir and serve immediately. Bean soup, potato soup, a beef stew — all of them will smile for you with this rich essence of yesterday's good times.

But there are other leftovers hanging around after holidays. Like the office Christmas present, a bottle of rye, which nobody in the house drinks. Scotch left over from visitors, heeltaps of gin and quarter bottles of wine. There's little point in keeping them, so use them. Take chicken legs fried in a little oil (just brown both sides) and sprinkle them with salt and pepper and a healthy spoonful of tarragon. Chop a clove of garlic and add that, then pour an ounce of rye over everything. Put the lid on, cook for another fifteen minutes and surprise yourself. Fry pork chops, add pepper, salt, thyme and garlic, fry a couple of minutes more, then add a sliced apple and a little rye. Cook with the lid on, stirring occasionally, until the apples have almost melted, pour in some more rye, bring it to a boil and serve immediately. There are, of course, people who don't drink rye, but they might not have a problem with leftover apple juice, which is a perfectly acceptable substitute for rye.

Chicken and gin is a wonderful dish. Just grate a little fresh ginger into the pan after you've browned the chicken, and a clove or two of garlic. Add the gin, a small piece of butter and a little chopped lemon peel. Pepper and salt and cook fifteen minutes, lid on, then sprinkle with lemon juice. Chicken and scotch? Just fry chicken until it's done, make sure everybody's at the table, pour an ounce of scotch into the hot pan and put a match to it. "Poof . . . ." You're a hero. And the slabs of leftover turkey? Cube them, fry them two minutes in a little oil then add a chopped onions, a clove of chopped garlic, some chopped celery, pepper, salt and a big pinch of cayenne pepper. Fry two minutes, then add two tablespoons peanut butter and the juice of a lemon. Stir it well, add just enough water (or chicken stock) to make a sauce, let it heat through and you have an African dish which nobody will recognize as the aftermath of Christmas dinner.

CHICKEN AND GIN

1 cut up chicken
3 - 4 slices fresh ginger
1 - 2 cloves garlic
lemon peel, chopped
butter
1 jigger of gin
salt and pepper

Brown the chicken and add some grated fresh ginger and the chopped garlic. Add the gin, a small piece of butter and a little chopped lemon peel. Season and cook for fifteen minutes with the lid on. Sprinkle with lemon juice and serve.

CHICKEN AND SCOTCH

1 cut up chicken
1 oz scotch

Fry the chicken until it is done. Pour the scotch into the hot pan and put a match to it.

TURKEY AFRICAN-STYLE

turkey leftovers
oil
1 onion, chopped
1 clove garlic, chopped
1 stick celery, chopped
2 tbsp peanut butter
juice of a lemon
salt and pepper
a good pinch of cayenne pepper
water or chicken stock

Cube the turkey and fry for 2 minutes in a little oil. Add the onion, garlic, celery, pepper, salt and cayenne pepper. Fry for a further 2 minutes then add the peanut butter and the lemon juice. Stir well and add just enough water or chicken stock to make a sauce. Heat it through and serve.

The Lowly Potato

It's nature's most unassuming vegetable, but that doesn't mean it has to be dull.

POTATO SOUP

4 medium potatoes
1 large onion, chopped
3 cloves garlic, finely
chopped
3 slices of bacon
1/4 tsp ground nutmeg
1/2 tsp pepper
salt

Cut the bacon into strips and cook slowly in a saucepan over low/medium heat. Don't crisp it. Stir in the chopped onion and the finely chopped garlic and cook slowly, stirring occasionally. Dice the unpeeled potatoes and when the onions are transparent stir in the potatoes, add four cups of hot water and simmer for 20 minutes. Add salt, pepper and ground nutmeg, cook for further 10 minutes and serve.

"Nothing much, dear — just meat and potatoes," said the Not So Confident Cook. "Nothing fancy, just meat and potatoes."

And right that very minute the phone rang. "You have just been elected," said a warm, comforting, peculiarly trustworthy voice, "to be Potato Queen of the Western World."

"Oh dear, oh dear," she said (and perfectly understandably, because in the circumstances you would probably say the same thing). "Why can't I be Peach Queen, or the Egg Lady — even Miss Lettuce? Potatoes are so *dull.*"

And right *that* very minute there was a great flash of light and the sound of thunder. The earth shook. "I didn't mean it!" she said (because nobody wants to incur the wrath of the Great Potato Fairy). "It's just that I don't know what to do with them."

But the thunder didn't stop. It was a truck dumping three tons of potatoes in her front driveway. The light was from a television crew arriving to shoot her inaugural speech.

This could happen to you. And you wouldn't want to stand there stuttering and dumb on the late night news, a self-proclaimed ignoramus, with the crown being wrested from your head by enraged potato farmers. So let's have a look at potatoes, which, like many wonderful things to eat, are considered dull in North America because they're not expensive. Buy some local potatoes, those nice medium-sized russets, peel them or scrub them and say to yourself (I wouldn't say it to anybody else because they might think you're not entirely on track), "I've got something really wonderful here and a bargain, too. Nice potato, good potato. Sit . . . ."

Four medium potatoes, a big brown-skinned onion, three cloves of garlic and three slices of bacon will make a magnificent half-hour soup for four on a cold, wet day. No stock, no soup cubes, just the lovely rich combination of bacon and potatoes. Cut the bacon crosswise into little strips and cook it slowly (low/medium heat) in a saucepan until the fat is running out. Don't crisp it. Stir in the onions and garlic, chopped fine, and cook slowly, stirring occasionally while you dice the potatoes (don't peel them; the skin will melt during the cooking and give the soup another dimension of flavour). When the onions are transparent, stir in the potatoes (get everything shiny with bacon), add four cups of hot water from the tap and simmer for 20 minutes. Add salt, a good half teaspoon of pepper and a big pinch (about a quarter teaspoon) of ground nutmeg. Cook another ten minutes and there's supper.

If you need to be fancy, stir in three or four tablespoons of heavy cream. If leeks are cheap, wash a couple well, chop them fine and add them at the same time as the onions. If the kids are hungry, dice some bread and fry it very slowly in a little oil or butter until all the sides are crispy and then sprinkle them over each bowl. If you're a vegetarian, or it's three days until payday, leave out the bacon and use oil, butter or lard to fry the onions. A bit of leftover ham, garlic sausage, the carcass of a chicken — there is no limit to what you can put into a potato soup. Add some grated vegetables and smoked sausage and you'll have a *garbure*. Whizz it in the food processor, let it get cold and stir in some cream and it's *vichyssoise*. Throw in a can of clams and some thyme and you have a wonderful chowder. Potatoes are infinitely adaptable once you have a couple of basic techniques.

French fries properly made are indescribably delicious, but despite all the fancy equipment now available to make them they are, to say the least, impractical for the average, non-commercial kitchen, particularly if it has kids, cats, dogs, a telephone or any of the usual distractions which don't mix at all well with boiling oil. But pan-fried potatoes (the fancy term is sautéed) are simpler and even more rewarding, as in, "Hey, this is *great!* Why don't we have this all the time?"

All you need is a frypan with a well fitting lid. The Greeks do this, the French, the Italians and now you. Cut the potato in half lengthwise and cut each half crosswise into three or four pieces. Heat three or four tablespoons of olive oil (medium/high heat) in the pan, add the potatoes and turn them over a couple of times to coat them well with the oil. Add two or three cloves of garlic, peeled and cut in half, and a teaspoon of dried sage leaves (or four or five fresh ones). Add salt and pepper to taste, put the lid on tight and let them steam in the juice that comes out of them, tossing occasionally. When they're tender (10, maybe 15 minutes), take the lid off, turn the heat up and lightly brown the outsides. Then they can sit and wait while you cook something else. In fact, they're even better served lukewarm, all soft and creamy inside and a little crusty outside.

You can do the same thing with thyme instead of sage and they'll be French potatoes. Use oregano for Greek, and if you want something indescribably rich and voluptuous, chop the garlic instead of slicing it and toss in half a dozen anchovy fillets instead of the herbs. The anchovies will melt, you toss the potatoes well to get the outside all

PAN-FRIED POTATOES, ITALIAN STYLE

3 medium potatoes
3 - 4 tbsp olive oil
2 - 3 cloves garlic, peeled and halved
1 tsp dried sage leaves (or 4 - 5 fresh ones)
salt and pepper

Cut each potato in half lengthwise and then each half crosswise into three or four pieces. Heat the oil in a frypan over medium/high heat. Add the potatoes and turn them a few times to coat with oil. Add the garlic, sage, salt and pepper and cook with the lid on tightly for about 10 - 15 minutes, tossing occasionally. When tender, remove the lid, turn the heat up and lightly brown the outsides.

FRENCH POTATOES

Make Pan-Fried Potatoes but substitute thyme for the sage.

GREEK POTATOES

Make Pan-Fried Potatoes but substitute oregano for the sage.

ANCHOVIES AND POTATOES

Make Pan-Fried Potatoes but chop the garlic instead of halving it and toss in half a dozen anchovy fillets instead of the herbs.

48

POTATO PANCAKES OR KARTOFFELPUFFERS

4 medium potatoes (or 2 large)
1 medium onion
3 - 4 tbsp oil (or lard)
2 eggs
1 cup flour
a good pinch of salt

Peel and coarsely grate the onion. Grate the potatoes and mix with the onion. Add the eggs, flour and salt and stir well together.

Heat the oil in a heavy frypan over medium/high heat and spoon in about 4 tablespoons of the mixture. Pat it down as thick as a hotcake and when the edges are brown and crisp, flip it over and cook the other side. Eat them hot with apple sauce and/or sour cream.

POTATOES AND MUSHROOMS (OR JANSSON'S FRESTELSE)

3 - 4 potatoes
2 tbsp oil
1/2 lb mushrooms
2 cloves garlic, roughly chopped
4 anchovy fillets
1/2 tsp salt
1/2 tsp pepper
1/2 tsp dried thyme or oregano

Cube the potatoes. Heat the oil in a heavy saucepan and toss the potatoes in it until they start to change color. Add the garlic and the anchovies and stir until the anchovies melt. Add the mushrooms whole if small, halved if larger and the seasonings. Toss everything together, put the lid on and cook for 15 minutes stirring occasionally.

For an additional delicacy add some dried orange peel along with the anchovies and garlic.

coated and then cook, as before, with the lid on. That's another technique. One recipe, five variations.

The Germans make potato pancakes, a wonderful weekend breakfast dish that's much easier than any conventional hotcake mix and the sort of recipe that will ensure you a permanent place in family history. If we called them *kartoffel-puffers* we might not make them, so let's just leave the name at potato pancakes. What you need is a couple of large or about four medium potatoes, a medium-sized onion, two eggs, a cup of flour and some salt. Peel the onion and grate it on the coarse side of the grater. Grate the potatoes and mix them into the onion. Then the eggs, the flour and a good pinch of salt, all well stirred together. Heat three or four tablespoons of oil (or, more traditionally, lard) in a heavy frypan (medium/high heat) and spoon in about four tablespoons of the mixture. Pat it down as thick as a hotcake and when the edges are nice and brown and crisp, flip it over and cook the other side. The edges will get browner than the middle, but that's the way they should be. Eat them hot with apple sauce and/or sour cream. With a big frypan or a griddle you will almost be able to keep up with the demand, but the really important thing is to make them so that *you* can be the one to sit and ask for more.

And finally, remember that potatoes and mushrooms have a natural affinity, like strawberries and cream or bacon and eggs. Cube three or four potatoes, heat two tablespoons of oil in a heavy saucepan and toss the potatoes in the hot oil until they're beginning to change colour. Now add a half pound of mushrooms — whole if they're small, halved if larger — and sprinkle with a half teaspoon salt, a half teaspoon pepper and at least half a teaspoon of dried thyme or oregano. Toss everything together, put the lid on and cook for fifteen minutes, stirring once or twice. This is the simple version, but to make it the very best potato dish you ever had, add four anchovy fillets just before you add the mushrooms and two cloves of garlic, rough-chopped. Stir until the anchovies melt. Then add the mushrooms and seasonings. What you will have is a simplified version of a Swedish dish called *Jansson's frestelse,* or Jansson's temptation. Once you've eaten it, you'll understand the name.

"What's for supper, dear?"

"Potatoes."

"Great. I'll tell the butler to get the candles. What time are the Rockefellers due?"

Everything You Ever Wanted To Know About Lamb

. . . but were afraid to ask.

In the old days, when the West was really Wild, when the Good Guys got the girls and the Bad Guys got run out of town by John Wayne, the cowboy hats were black or they were white. There were no compromises. Men were men and women were Miss Emily, kinda purty and a good hand with a pie.

Cowboy songs, cowboy boots, jeans, beans and the Wild Night on the Town — the western myth grew big and strong on a steady diet of chauvinism and steak. Beef *was* the West — "a man's gotta chew what a man's gotta chew . . ." — and the cameras, while they never actually shot cooking shows, were very important in determining our North American diet.

The red-blooded Real Men, who spent their days in the saddle tamping the thundering herds, could hardly be expected to eat vegetables. Good Guys or Bad Guys, they both ate steak, and the Real Women, in their patched and faded sugar sack dresses, savin' a few pennies from th' egg money to buy little Melinda a piano somewhere down the line, stood by their men (or perhaps a little behind them), sharing their hopes, their dreams, and above all their hatred for them panty-waisted softies — the sheepherders.

Lamb got a lot of bad press in the westerns, from which it's only recently recovered. Sissies, wimps, city slickers, school marms and *furriners* ate lamb and we sure didn't want to be none of them. Even when we reached the age of choice, and could stop eating what was good for us, when we discovered that we actually *liked* spinach and that garlic wasn't detectable at 400 yards, our early cultural associations were so strong that we still couldn't order lamb without shame. Only last year a syndicated newspaper columnist seriously advised aspiring hosts to call their guests in advance and "discreetly inquire" as to whether lamb was "appropriate."

I was raised on lamb. A leg on Sundays, roasted. Cold lamb on Mondays (very nice, actually, with pickled onions and good bread). Shepherd's pie on Tuesdays (and still a favourite for a family supper). Curried lamb on Wednesdays and what my mother called mince on Thursdays — all the scraps not cooked in the other dishes put through

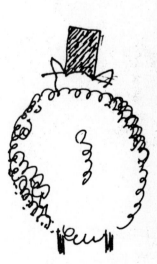

ROAST LAMB AND ANCHOVIES

1 lamb loin, rib roast or rack
2 cloves garlic, chopped
1 small can anchovies
(including the oil)
2 tbsp brown sugar or honey
a pinch of cayenne pepper

*Carve a diamond pattern
into the fat of the roast using
the point of a sharp knife,
making the cuts about half
an inch apart and a quarter
of an inch deep.
Mix the garlic, anchovies
and oil, brown sugar or
honey and cayenne pepper.
Rub this mixture all over the
lamb making sure you push
it well into the cuts. Put the
roast, bone side down, into a
oven pre-heated to 400°F.
Baste it after five, ten then
twenty minutes and then turn
down the oven to 350°F.
Cook for about 20 - 25
minutes a pound. Remove
from oven and let it rest for 5
- 10 minutes before serving.*

the grinder and mixed with grated carrots, onions and rosemary. It wasn't really lamb we ate. It was mutton, a giant leg from some ancient sheep which could no longer get through its aerobic classes.

Today's lamb is very different. Legs come on the bone or boneless, chops come in racks or in packets of two (just right for the unmarried frypan) and all the other bits and pieces, shanks, ribs, shoulders and breasts are packaged, with the fat trimmed, in the right-sized pieces for cooking. Most of this packaged and pre-cut lamb is from New Zealand — sometimes it's frozen — and since all the supermarkets stock it, they're good places to begin an understanding of lamb. Restaurants use a lot of New Zealand lamb because it saves extra messing in the kitchen and keeps their costs down. The Australians are desperately trying to catch up to New Zealand in the lamb business, but they've still got a long way to go.

Then there's local lamb, which is nearly always fresh (meaning not frozen). To get it you usually have to go to a butcher, an independent, small shop specialist who gets enthusiastic. Or you buy a whole lamb. Whichever way you do it, unless you're a surgeon, you'll finish up with a butcher cutting it for you. Local lamb is expensive, but fresh and unique in its flavour, just as local strawberries or tomatoes fresh off the vine have a special, indefinable *something* about them.

Whatever lamb you get, you'll want to cook it. It doesn't have to be the most expensive cut, but if you want to entertain friends or simply overindulge your own two selves, try lamb and anchovies. Take a loin, a rib roast or a rack and crisscross the fat into half-inch diamonds about ¼-inch deep with the point of a sharp knife.

Crush and chop two cloves of garlic and mix them in a bowl with a small can of anchovies, oil and all. Add two tablespoons of brown sugar or honey and a pinch of red cayenne pepper. Stir the mixture smooth with a wooden spoon and then rub it into the criss-crosses on the lamb. Push it into the cuts, rub the ends, and generally cover the lamb with this gucky brown mixture. Heat the oven to 400°F and put the roast in, bone side down. Baste it after five, ten and twenty minutes (you may need an extra spoonful of oil to do this), then turn the oven down to 350°F. Total cooking time is between 20 and 25 minutes a pound. Take it out of the oven and let it rest for five or ten minutes while you cook zucchini or other vegetables, and there's dinner, dark brown as a chestnut and fragrant (maybe *aromatic* is the word we need here), the lamb pink on the inside and each chop with its own little bone handle so you can suck on it. So will your family, friends, guests, business associates, lovers and members of your investment club. "Lamb," they'll murmur. "Never knew it could taste this good."

If you put half a dozen medium-sized onions in the pan when the lamb goes in — nice, firm, shiny-skinned ordinary brown onions in their skins — they will become slightly caramelized, soft and sweet on the inside. Add a little pepper just before you eat them and you have a taste of old time kitchens and wood fires. Lovely.

That's high society lamb. But there are inexpensive cuts which make extraordinarily good stews, many of which are never made because they have fancy names or sound complicated. Lamb stews are subtler and richer than beef stews — and all the other ingredients get a chance to say how nice they are.

Lamb is the meat of country people — people who ate what grew around them when it was ripe, and learned to do without refrigeration or expensive imports. Country people make simple dishes, which the fancy magazines feel obliged to improve on, never quite understanding the virtue (or the wonderful taste) of the original simplicity.

Try this. Sometimes called *chelo* and sometimes *polo,* it has a lovely rich and sophisticated taste, and there's nothing in it that you can't get at the supermarket. Make it first, then decide what you're going to call it. Heat two tablespoons of oil over medium/high heat and fry one and a half pounds of lean lamb, cut into one-inch cubes. When the meat is light brown all over, add one ounce of butter (it gives a nice nutty flavour) and one onion chopped fine. Turn the heat to medium/low and cook until the onions are soft, stirring frequently. Add half a teaspoon salt, the same of cinnamon. Now add three heaping tablespoons of fat, seedless sultannas, and four to six ounces of dried apricots. There are two kinds of apricots in the stores, one sweet, the other sharp. Sharp tastes better. Stir everything together, add water to cover and simmer gently on top of the stove for 1½ to 2 hours. If it looks soupy, take out the meat and fruit and boil the sauce down. Then recombine it.

That's the basic dish, hardly any work and very simple. I like to serve it with fresh lemon juice (a cut quarter on each plate) and sprinkled with almonds fried just brown and then crushed. If you have fresh mint in the garden, a few leaves chopped and mixed into thin-sliced fresh mushrooms tossed in plain yogurt make a very suitable side dish. And if you cook rice with a whole, unpeeled caradamom and a good dollop of butter added to the water, you will be three quarters of the way to heaven. But you don't *need* all these fancies — not when plain and simple and quick and hardly any work all add up to wonderful.

CHELO OR POLO OR LAMB AND APRICOTS

1-1/2 lb lean lamb, cut into one-inch cubes
2 tbsp oil
1 oz butter
1 onion, finely chopped
3 heaped tbsp seedless sultana raisins
4 - 6 oz dried apricots
1/2 tsp salt
1/2 tsp ground pepper
1/2 tsp cinnamon

Heat the oil over medium/high heat and fry the cubed lamb. When light brown, add the butter and onion and cook over a medium/low heat until the onions are soft. Add the salt, pepper and cinnamon. Now add the sultanas and apricots, stir everything together, add water to cover and simmer gently on top of the stove for 1 1/2 - 2 hours. Serve with fresh lemon juice and lemon quarters.

Chicken Ad Lib

The first rule of the kitchen is to use your imagination.

Kids learn to paint when they're little tads, and their daubs ("That's just lovely, Christopher!") get hung on refrigerator doors, in laundry rooms and on the office walls of the truly secure. Kids paint the way they paint until the very moment somebody starts to tell them how. "What's it s'posed to *be*?" says somebody, and nine times out of ten it starts to be anything but the spontaneous, colourful and imaginative mess it was when the two-year-old brain waves were just flowing out of the fingertips. Pretty soon somebody else says, "Paper costs money, you know." And that's the end of another era — there just aren't so many paintings anymore. Ten years down the road the colours in most kids' minds have faded to drab and *art* is another boring and unreal subject, hung on walls to impress people.

Chicken is the finger paint of the kitchen. There is nothing cheaper or more readily and regularly available. And for people who want to escape the boredom of cooking or the tyranny of The Only Six Things My Family Will Eat, a reversion to the pleasures and irresponsibilities of childhood is right there on the meat counter, waving its wings and just begging for a chance at the big time.

Shake'n'Bake is not the answer to being a good cook, any more than paint-by-numbers kits will turn you into a Picasso. Chicken lends itself to improvisation, to something out of your head rather than out of a packet. So let's improvise in the simplest way we can — on top of the stove in a frypan.

Legs, wings, breasts and thighs, in big pieces or cut small, with the bones in or without — it's all chicken, pieces of chicken , and the larger the pieces the longer they will take to cook. We dust these pieces with a little cornstarch, heat about two tablespoons of oil in the frypan and fry the chicken over medium/high heat until the outsides have all changed colour. No flavourings, no pepper, no salt. Not yet. Now add a chopped onion, large, small or medium. The size is not important — and it's not *s'posed* to be *anything*. It's *your* chicken. Stir it all about a bit until it smells nice and round. What does round smell like? Sort of sugary, maybe nutty, like frying onions — you know. Then add a sprinkle of salt. How much is a sprinkle? Ask your four-year-old. And a smaller sprinkle of pepper, unless you really like pepper. Then you add a larger sprinkle of pepper.

That's the basic part. Now we can start to improvise. Want to be French? Try *poulet Veronique*. Add a handful of seedless grapes to the pan and two or three big pinches of tarragon. Stir it all about so that everything in the pan gets to know everything else. Cook for four minutes if they're small pieces, longer if they're larger and then dump it all out onto a good looking dish. Add half a cup of white wine or apple juice to the pan, turn up the heat and boil it down until it's nearly all gone. That's the sauce, which you pour over the chicken and grapes.

Instead of the grapes, add oranges, peeled and separated into sections. Mandarins are nice, but big oranges work just as well — you just have to cut the sections in half. Tarragon is good with oranges, so is thyme, so is basil. White wine or apple juice, just as before, and you have *poulet Mandarin*.

That's a start. Now let's get really exotic. Cut three or four rashers of bacon crosswise into matchstick bits and fry them in a dry pan on medium heat until the fat comes out. Add the chicken (dusted with a little cornstarch, just as before), then a diced potato. Stir it well together over medium/high heat and then add the chopped onion, the pepper (there should be enough salt in the bacon), a large pinch of thyme and a bay leaf if you've got one. A chopped clove of garlic is a good thing right now (or two or three) and a few fresh mushrooms, quartered unless they're small enough to cook whole.

Stir it all well and add half a cup (about a quarter of a bottle) of beer. Or apple juice, or chicken stock. Put the lid on and let it cook. Small pieces of chicken will take ten minutes, larger pieces about twenty. *Poulet bonne femme,* it's s'posed to be called.

Instead of grapes, or oranges, or potatoes, use quartered and sliced apples, which will turn it into a *poulet Normande*. For a lovely, rich German-style dish, fry the chicken pieces a bit (same basic procedure as before) and then add two, even three onions, sliced thin. Pepper well and salt cautiously, then add a teaspoon of caraway seeds. A little beer, instead of white wine or apple juice, but everything else is the same as in the first recipe.

That's four recipes: *poulet Verronique, poulet bonne femme, poulet Normande* and *poulet Allemande.* You may now realize that if you haven't got grapes or apples or mandarins, pears will do just as well. Or peaches, or those thin green beans cut into little finger lengths, or cut up cabbage, or diced green peppers. And if you haven't got chicken, then pork will do just as well. A pork steak or a piece of pork shoulder cut up into small pieces and the chicken recipes.

"What's that called, Mum?"

"Er . . . pork Veronique."

No pork? Then use turkey meat. This is finger painting, where the

CHICKEN VARIATIONS

BASIC RECIPE

chicken pieces
1 onion, chopped
2 tbsp oil
cornstarch
salt and pepper

Dust the chicken pieces with cornstarch. Heat the oil in a frypan and fry the chicken over medium/high heat until the outsides have all changed color. Add the onion and stir until cooked through. Add salt and pepper.

CHICKEN VERONIQUE

a handful of seedless grapes
2 - 3 large pinches of tarragon
1/2 cup white wine or apple juice

Add the grapes and tarragon to the above chicken and stir it together well. Cook for 4 minutes. Remove onto serving plate. Pour the white wine or apple juice into the pan, turn up the heat and boil it down until it's nearly gone. Pour over the chicken and grapes.

CHICKEN MANDARIN

2 - 3 oranges or mandarins
2 - 3 large pinches of tarragon, thyme or basil
1/2 cup white wine or apple juice

Peel and separate the oranges or mandarins into sections. Cook as for Chicken Veronique, substituting the oranges for the grapes.

CHICKEN NORMANDE

2 - 3 apples, quartered and sliced
2 - 3 large pinches of thyme or sage
1/2 cup white wine, dry cider or apple juice

Cook as for Chicken Veronique, substituting the apples for the grapes.

CHICKEN ALLEMANDE

2 - 3 onions, sliced thin
1 tsp caraway seeds
1/2 cup beer

Cook as for Chicken Veronique, substituting onions for the grapes, caraway seeds for the tarragon and beer for the wine.

CHICKEN BONNE FEMME

3 - 4 slices of bacon
1 potato, diced
1 onion, chopped
a few fresh mushrooms
2 - 3 cloves of garlic, chopped
1 large pinch of thyme
1 bay leaf
1/2 cup of beer, apple juice or chicken stock
pepper

Cut the bacon into matchstick strips and fry them over medium/high heat. Add the chicken, dusted with cornstarch, and the diced potato. Stir well and add the chopped onion, pepper, mushrooms (quartered unless small enough to be whole), garlic, thyme and the bay leaf. Stir well and add the beer, apple juice or chicken stock. Put the lid on and cook for about 10 minutes if the chicken pieces are small or 20 minutes if larger.

supremely confident, totally imaginative cook takes off the training wheels and goes solo. Pretty soon you'll be learning that recipes which call for lemon juice usually work well with orange or even grapefruit juice. You'll just *know* when things ought to have more garlic than the recipe calls for, just as you'll know that clarified butter is more fuss than it's worth for everyday cooking, and that peanut oil tastes nice — not the same as olive oil, but nice. Just different.

And most of all, you'll learn that the only thing cooking is *s'posed* to do is give you pleasure.

Cheese — Milk's Leap Toward Immortality

A lump of cheese is a good thing to have in the fridge, even if you *don't* have mice in your basement. Cooked or raw, grated, sliced or just broken off in chunks, it goes with almost everything from pickled onions to spaghetti. It fits equally well into lunchboxes, brown paper bags or pants pockets, it keeps well, it can be sat on without ruining its complexion, and since there's no waste, no bones, it's reasonably inexpensive.

I'm talking about *real* cheese, the stuff that comes in pieces, not slices — Canadian cheddar, rough on the tongue and rich in the burp. Cheese that crumbles, cheese that won't bend in the heat of a hamburger, cheese that will grate, cheese that will chew — cheese that *won't* melt in your mouth. Just good, honest, plain cheese.

The best cheese dishes are the simple ones. And frequently, because they are so simple and so inexpensive, the recipes go out of circulation. They're just not *fancy* enough. Take macaroni and cheese, that good old standby of the '30s that families ate once a week. Everybody loved macaroni and cheese. Leftovers got fried up the next morning for breakfast, diners served it as a daily special, and prairie hotel menus, sprinkled with fancy French names (a sign of class), managed to slide *macaroni au fromage* just before the *salade de lettuce du jour.*

Macaroni and cheese was not too popular to attract imitators, and too basically simple to survive them. Kraft dinner first made it easy and finally made it obsolete. Not even the most depraved of teenaged appetites snuck into the fridge to grab a piece of cold Kraft dinner. Fettucine Alfredo took its place in the fancier restaurants and Mom and Pop, when they sold the diner, didn't include any recipes.

But its memory lingers on. Just whisper, "Macaroni and cheese" in any family, even one without a grandmother, and eyes fill with rose-coloured tears of nostalgia. I'm surprised that nobody's made a television series called *Macaroni and Cheese.* People that you know full well were raised on cold pizza and Cheesies for breakfast and don't know a cow from a goose will tell you interminable stories of life on the farm, the Hungry Thirties and their grandmother's ability to make

MACARONI AND CHEESE

2 cups short macaroni
3 tbsp butter
1 large onion, coarsely chopped
8 oz fresh mushrooms, sliced
1 medium green pepper, chopped,
or 2 medium tomatoes, chopped
2 tbsp flour
1 tsp dry mustard
1/2 tsp salt
1/2 tsp dried (or 2 sprigs fresh) oregano
2 - 3 cups milk
8 oz cheddar cheese, coarsely grated
a good pinch of cayenne pepper or two good pinches of chili powder
a big handful of dry breadcrumbs

Drop the macaroni into boiling water and cook for 10 - 15 minutes. When tender, drain and put into a well-buttered, three-quart casserole.

Whilst cooking, pre-heat the oven to 350°F and melt the butter in a frypan over medium heat. Toss the vegetables in the pan until just tender and stir in the flour, mustard, salt and oregano. Add the milk slowly, half a cup at a time, stirring continuously. When this sauce is heated through and thickened, slowly add more milk and stir in the cayenne pepper and 6 oz of cheese until melted.

Pour everything over the macaroni and stir a couple of times. Mix the breadcrumbs and remaining cheese together and sprinkle on the top. Cook for 45 minutes. The top should be bubbling and crispy (this can be done under the broiler if necessary). Serve immediately.

a graduation dress out of flour sacks.

Macaroni, dropped into boiling water, takes between ten and fifteen minutes to cook. As soon as it's tender, drain it and put it in a good, big (three-quart) casserole, well buttered. While it's cooking and the oven's heating to 350°F, get your good, big frypan and over medium heat toss the vegetables in the butter until they're just tender. Stir in the flour, mustard, salt and oregano, and slowly, half a cup at a time, add the two cups of milk, stirring continuously, which will make a sauce.

When the sauce is heated through and thickened, slowly add more milk until it is just a little thicker than heavy cream. Stir in the cayenne pepper and 6 ounces of the cheese until it is all melted. Then pour everything over the macaroni, stirring it all together once or twice. Any milk left over you will, of course, give to the cat, because all good macaroni and cheese households have a fat, milk-loving cat, just like the one they had on the farm.

Mix the breadcrumbs and remaining cheese together and sprinkle evenly over the top. Cook for 45 minutes and if the top is brown, serve immediately. If it isn't brown, turn on the broiler and crisp the top for a couple of minutes, until it's nice and bubbly and crusty.

It should be just right for six people with a fresh and simple "eat your greens" salad on the side. Resist all other attempts to improve it — unless you slip in two big pinches of nutmeg with the dried mustard.

Pan Haggerty is another utterly simple country dish which can earn you a reputation with nothing more than potatoes, cheese and an onion. In fancy neighbourhoods it would be known as a *gratin* and served in delicate, little portions, but I prefer it in large slices for supper. This recipe makes enough for four healthy appetites.

Wash a couple (about a pound) of good, firm potatoes — don't peel them — and slice them as thin as you possibly can (the single slicing slot on the side of a grater works well). Put them immediately into a big bowl of cold water, slosh them around a bit to wash off the starch and dry them on a tea towel. Peel the onions, slice them thin and separate the rings. Grate about four ounces of cheddar cheese.

Melt a couple of tablespoons of butter in an eight- or nine-inch frypan. Take it off the heat and build the ingredients in the pan. First a layer of potato slices, slightly overlapping. Then a layer of onion rings and finally a layer of cheese. A little salt, a bit more pepper, and then do it again, finishing with a layer of potatoes. Put the pan back on low/medium heat and cook about eight minutes. Then turn the heat up a bit to brown the bottom.

Put a plate over the pan and quickly flip it over. Add a bit more butter and slide the pan haggerty back into the pan, cooked side up. Cook another eight to 10 minutes, slide it out onto a plate and supper's ready.

Very simple, very filling.

Then there are tricks like mashing potatoes with grated cheese instead of butter, adding a little chopped parsley for colour and a little finely chopped onion for flavour. Fluff them up with a fork and look clever. If there are any leftovers next day, beat an egg or two in and roll a spoonful at a time into a little sausage. Roll each sausage in breadcrumbs and pan-fry them until the outsides are a good nutty brown.

And then, of course, there's Welsh rarebit, the finest of all cheese dishes, magnificently indigestible and very, very simple. Slowly melt two tablespoons of butter in a heavy saucepan (it will burn in a lightweight pan). Add four ounces of grated cheddar cheese and stir it while it melts — just enough to keep it from turning into a great lump. As it melts, sprinkle in one tablespoon of flour, one teaspoon of mustard powder, one teapoon of paprika and a fair shake of pepper, stirring continuously. Just about this time you delegate someone else to start making toast.

Still stirring, slowly pour in most of a bottle of beer. The Welsh rarebit will turn into a thick and sticky sludge. Turn off the heat, quickly slide in a whole egg and stir furiously. Serve it immediately. How much salt you need will depend on how much salt there is in the cheese.

And one more thing. All those pieces of leftover cheese you have, going dry in the fridge: once a month or so, dump them all in the food processor with a quarter pound of butter, a little dry mustard, some chopped onions if you like, a little parsley maybe and some paprika if you have it. Whizz it all together until its smooth. Put it in a jar and use it for sandwiches, mashing potatoes, melting on vegetables, spreading on toast and melting in the toaster oven, stuffing celery or, in a pinch, as earplugs when the kids next door have a party.

And remember, if you do have mice, what they *really* like is bacon.

PAN HAGGERTY

1 lb potatoes, washed
2 - 3 large onions
4 oz cheddar cheese, grated
2 tbsp butter
salt and pepper

Slice the unpeeled potatoes as thin as possible and put them immediately into cold water. Dry on a towel. Peel and slice the onions thinly and separate the rings.

Melt the butter in an 8" - 9" frypan, remove from heat and build layers of potato and onion. Slightly overlapping potatoes first, then onion rings, then a layer of cheese, some salt, some pepper and then repeat. Finish with a layer of potatoes. Return the pan to a low/medium heat and cook about 8 minutes.

Turn the heat up and brown the bottom. Put a plate over the pan and flip it over. Add more butter and slide the pan haggerty back into the pan - cooked side up. Cook for a further 8 minutes and serve.

WELSH RAREBIT

2 tbsp butter
4 oz cheddar cheese, grated
1 tbsp flour
1 tsp mustard powder
1 tsp paprika
a good pinch of pepper
1 bottle of beer
1 egg

Slowly melt the butter in a heavy saucepan. Add the cheese and stir whilst it melts. Sprinkle in the flour, mustard, paprika and pepper, stirring continuously. Still stirring, slowly pour in most of a bottle of beer. As it turns thick and sticky, turn off the heat, quickly slide in an egg and stir furiously. Serve immediately on some toast.

Oodles Of Noodles

Unravelling the mysteries of pasta.

**FETTUCCINE
PRIMAVERA**

550 gm fettuccine
1 medium red onion,
coarsely chopped
large handful snow peas
half a dozen small carrots
choice of some or all of the
following:

small cauliflower,
cut into florets
2 zucchini, sliced
250 gm mushrooms,
sliced
1 red or green pepper,
coarsely chopped
a dozen stalks asparagus,
cut into one-inch lengths
a dozen cherry tomatoes
broccoli, cut into florets
a bunch of green onions,
cut into one-inch lengths
4 tbsp olive oil
1/2 tsp salt
1/2 tsp pepper
1 heaped tsp dried, or fresh
basil, finely chopped
1/2 cup heavy cream
parmesan (or asiago)
cheese, grated
parsley, chopped

*Put the peas and carrots into
a large pot of boiling, salted
water and cook for 2
minutes. Remove with a
slotted spoon and run under
a cold tap.*

Fat and skinny, long and short or straight and curly — pasta comes in as many shapes and sizes as people and is as frequently misunderstood. Doctors have fancy names for different body types — skinnies are *ectomorphs* and the biggies *endomorphs* — but normal people don't use those kinds of words to talk about their acquaintances. They describe them in more familiar terms, like "string bean," "pear shape," "dumpling" or "pork chop," all words we don't have to think very hard about to understand.

Pasta is like that in Italy. Those strange words we find on packets and in fancy recipes, words like *orrecchiette* or *rotini,* are all essentially words for pasta. They're mostly interchangeable. A recipe won't be ruined if you use *penne rigate* instead of *rigatoni,* or even plain old spaghetti. *Orrechiette* means little ears, and *rotini* means screws — that's what they look like so that's what they're called.

So don't worry. Pasta is pasta. Thick pasta takes longer to cook than thin, and big pasta needs a big sauce. Small pasta takes light sauces and sometimes butter and pepper is enough. And that's it. That's all there is to the secret of pasta, and now that the big pasta fashion rush is over and nice normal people can get back to eating it without worrying about the gourmet police breaking down the door, we can get on with cooking it.

One more thing. There's nothing wrong with dried pasta. It isn't inferior to fresh, homemade pasta. It's just different. And sometimes it's preferable to fresh, particularly if you want to make a great big spicy sauce and need pasta to support it on the perilous journey between the bowl and your face. And if you want to make a cold pasta salad (just cook twice as much as you can eat and keep half of it until tomorrow), you will find that dried pasta not only holds up better (it doesn't look as though it's spent the night sleeping on the chesterfield) but also picks up better and somehow even increases the flavour of your dressing.

Let's start with the simplest of sauces, pasta primavera. In the spring, when all the new little vegetables come to market, good Italian families make this pasta primavera, or springtime pasta. You can do it, courtesy of the supermarkets, most of the year. Just make sure everything is fresh — this is not a catch-all recipe for the day you clean out the fridge.

A large pot of boiling, salted water is the first essential and, for four people, about 550 grams of fettucine. If you can buy half green fettuccine and half plain, the two colours cooked together make a nice contrast, what the Italians call "straw and hay."

Now you'll need some vegetables, like a nice medium-sized red onion, a big handful of snow peas and half a dozen of those nice small carrots. Put the peas and the carrots into the boiling water and let them cook for two minutes, no more. Fish them out with a slotted spoon and run them under the cold tap until they're cold.

Now you have a choice — all or any half-dozen of the following: a small cauliflower broken into small flowers; a couple of sliced zucchini; 250 grams of mushrooms, sliced; a green pepper or a red one or both, coarsely chopped; a dozen or so stalks of asparagus cut into one-inch lengths; a dozen cherry tomatoes; broccoli separated into flowers the same size as the cauliflower; and a bunch of green onions cut into one-inch lengths. Have them ready and cut, the onion in lumps as big as a walnut. And you will also need to chop some parsley.

Dried pasta will take about 12 minutes to cook, fresh about two. The sauce will take exactly five from the time the pan is hot, so figure out when to start it (a good job for the children). Heat four tablespoons of olive oil in a large frypan over medium/high heat. Stir-fry the green onions and asparagus (if you're using it) for one minute, add half a teaspoon of salt and all the other vegetables for a garnish, add the snow peas and carrots to the pan and cook one minute. Add half a cup of heavy cream, half a teaspoon of pepper and a heaped teaspoon of dried or a handful of fresh, finely chopped basil. Toss it all well together and cook one minute more.

Drain the pasta well, pour the vegetables over it and toss. Add the vegetables kept for a garnish, sprinkle well with grated parmesan or Asiago (cheaper) cheese and finish with a dusting of chopped parsley. This is a wonderful dish served hot, but it can also be made a couple of hours beforehand, loosely covered and left at room temperature until you serve it.

Even quicker is this recipe using the same pasta, a pound of fresh, thinly sliced mushrooms, pepper, salt and a half teaspoon of nutmeg. Sprinkle the mushrooms with salt and cook them in butter for two minutes. Then add the pepper, nutmeg and half a cup of heavy cream. Cook another two minutes and pour over the pasta. Garnish with a little chopped parsley. If you're a microwaver, simply cook everything except the parsley and pasta together in a dish and then pour it over the pasta.

Cook the pasta in the boiling, salted water for 12 minutes, if dried, and 2 minutes, if fresh.

Heat the oil in a large frypan over medium/high heat. Stir-fry the green onions and asparagus for 1 minute. Add the salt and all the other vegetables and stir-fry for 3 minutes. Remove about a quarter of the vegetables for a garnish, add the peas and carrots and cook for 1 minute. Add the cream, pepper and basil. Toss all together and cook 1 minute more.

Drain the pasta, pour the vegetables over it and toss. Add the vegetables reserved for garnish, sprinkle well with the parmesan and finish with a dusting of chopped parsley.

FETTUCCINE WITH MUSHROOMS

550 gm fettuccine
1 lb fresh mushrooms, thinly sliced
pepper and salt
1/2 tsp nutmeg
butter
1/2 cup heavy cream
parsley, chopped

Cook the pasta in a large pot of boiling, salted water as above and drain well.

Sprinkle the mushrooms with salt and cook them in butter for 2 minutes. Add the pepper, nutmeg and cream and cook for further 2 minutes. Pour over the pasta and garnish with parsley.

FETTUCCINE WITH TUNA

550 gm fettuccine
1 can tuna
1 onion, chopped
2 ripe tomatoes, coarsely chopped
4 tbsp capers
juice of a lemon
1 heaped tsp oregano
pepper

Fry the onion over medium/high heat along with a generous amount of pepper. Add the tuna, tomatoes, capers, oregano and lemon juice and stir gently. Cook for 2 minutes, pour over the pasta (cooked as above) and serve hot or cold.

SPAGHETTI WITH OIL AND GARLIC

550 gm spaghetti
1 large head garlic, separated into cloves but not peeled
1/4 cup olive oil
1 heaped tsp pepper

Cook the garlic cloves in the oil over medium heat, stirring occasionally, until the skins are light brown. Squash a few of the cloves with the back of a spoon, add the pepper and pour over the pasta, including the oil.

The quickest recipe of all calls for the same pasta and a can of tuna. Chop an onion, dust it copiously with pepper (be more than generous) and fry it two minutes over medium/high heat. Add the tuna, two ripe, coarsely chopped tomatoes and four tablespoons of capers. Stir gently, add a big teaspoon of oregano and the juice of a lemon. Cook two minutes and serve hot or cold. This is a very basic southern Italian recipe which makes good leftovers.

If you want to be utterly simple and extraordinarily adventurous, try spaghetti with oil and garlic. One big head of garlic, separated into cloves but not peeled, will do for a start, but next time you'll want to use two heads. Put a quarter cup of good olive oil in a pan over medium heat and cook the garlic, stirring occasionally, until the skins are light brown. (Garlic cooked in its skin doesn't burn like peeled garlic.) Squash a few of the cloves with the back of a spoon, add a good, big teaspoon of pepper, pour everything over the pasta and eat. Pasta shouldn't scare you.

The Plight Of The Patty

Hamburger doesn't need to be dull.
It's up to you
to give it the break it deserves.

My first cookbook was a child born of sadness and hamburger. Too many times I'd seen ground beef dumped into a pan, stirred with apathy and a fork until it turned grey, doused with ketchup and eaten standing at the stove from the pan it was cooked in. I'd seen men, women and youngsters do it, all of them quietly proud that they couldn't cook.

The hamburger is such a North American dish, such an essential part of our folklore. Hamburgers, like popcorn, convertibles and coeds, are bettter known than the maple leaf or the Statue of Liberty. I once knew a woman, spoilt and rich. She'd never cooked, never even picked up her own clothes, and she came to Canada for a new life. She was going to support herself, work and be a normal person. She knew about hamburgers, and every Sunday night she bought seven Big Macs. One she ate, the others she froze. Every night at 6 PM she melted the frost off one of them and ate it — not out of laziness, but as a statement of faith like saluting the flag or singing the anthem, a ritual which silently swore an irrevocable allegiance to a new culture. In the end she got bored and went back to the butler and the dinners that just arrived, no questions asked, on the table every night. I never figured out if it was Canada, the hamburgers or the poverty which eventually drove her away, but I like to blame it on the hamburgers, which in their normal, commercial or domestic form are so unnecessarily *boring*.

The first thing you must learn to do is stretch it. Even the Simple Simon, throw-it-on-the-barbecue patty is vastly improved by mixing it with a handful of rolled oats, a finely chopped onion, an egg and some rosemary. The French add nutmeg, the Greeks oregano, and the Italians make a wonderful rice-wrapped hamburger called *arancini*. The Chinese steam theirs (using pork, not beef) and in Yugoslavia ground lamb becomes a sausage-shaped hamburger called *cevapcici*. *Boulettes* they're called in the French countryside, and Salisbury steak in England. All of these, whatever the name and whatever the ingredients, are infinitely more exciting than the unadorned, 100 percent meat hamburger patty that lurks inside the average bun.

HAMBURGER SANDWICH

1 1/2 lb ground beef
1/2 lb ground pork
1 1/2 tsp salt
1 tsp pepper
1 onion, finely chopped
2 tsp chili powder
juice of half a lemon
2 slices bread, soaked in water and squeezed
2 tbsp butter

Mix the beef, pork, 1 tsp salt and the pepper. Divide the mixture into eight parts and flatten each one into rounds.

Mix together the onion, chili powder, lemon juice, bread, salt and butter. Put this mixture in four of the rounds and cover with the others. Press the edges tightly together and barbecue over a medium fire, turning once.

HAMBURGER FRENCH STYLE

1 lb ground beef
1 medium onion, finely chopped
1 egg
1 tsp pepper
1/2 tsp nutmeg
1/2 tsp aniseed
1 tsp salt or 3 anchovy fillets, finely chopped

Mix all the ingredients together with your hands and make into thick patties, well-patted all over. Brush with oil to barbecue or dust with flour to fry.

HAMBURGER SCOTTISH-STYLE

1 lb ground beef
1 onion, chopped
1 tsp pepper
1 tsp salt
1/2 tsp dry mustard powder
2 eggs
1/2 cup rolled oats

Mix all the ingredients and make the patties thinner than usual. Pat a little more oatmeal onto each side before frying.

So let's start with the usual pound of ground beef. Add it to one medium onion, finely chopped, one egg, one teaspoon of pepper, a half teaspoon of nutmeg, a half teaspoon of salt or three anchovy fillets, finely chopped. Mix it well. Squish it in a bowl with your hands, and make it into thick patties, well-patted all over. Brush with oil to barbecue or dust with flour to fry. That's a very French hamburger, moist and very flavourful. The anchovy melts and disappears but leaves the hamburger with a distinct, nutty, non-anchovy flavour. In Scotland, for economy and texture, they use ground beef, chopped onion, pepper and salt, a half teaspoon of dry mustard powder, two eggs and half a cup of rolled oats. They make the patties thinner than usual, and then pat a little more oatmeal onto each side before frying, which gives them a nice, toasted flavour.

The Greeks make small hamburgers called *keftedes* using ground beef, a finely chopped onion, three to four cloves of chopped garlic, a big handful of chopped parsley, a few mint leaves, half a teaspoon of cinnamon and one egg. They extend the meat with a couple of slices of good bread, soaked in water and then squeezed dry. They mix everything together, add a good teaspoon of pepper and a little salt and then knead it all on a board for a couple of minutes until it's soft and pliable. Putting it in the fridge for an hour or two at this stage will make it easy to handle. Pinch off lumps as big as walnuts and roll them into balls between your palms (kids love to do this). Roll them in flour and fry in hot oil, moving them constantly until they're crisp and brown. Made with lean ground lamb instead of beef they're even nicer, and made smaller (a bit bigger than marbles) they're just right for tucking into a split pita bread with a little yogurt — instant souvlaki.

In Yugoslavia every village has its own way of making hamburgers, but the basic starting point is to always use two kinds of meat — half pork, half beef or lamb. Regardless of which are used, the hamburgers are called *cevapcici*. I like to use a pound of meat, a medium onion, a teaspoon of paprika, the zest (the thin, yellow outside peel) of a lemon, very finely chopped, two slices of bread (soaked and squeezed), a clove of garlic and a little salt. Squish everything together and roll it into thumb-sized pieces. Fry them until they're brown all over and serve them with a salad of raw, chopped onion, liberally peppered and splashed with vinegar.

But if you want a monster, reputation-making, party-sized hamburger, there's nothing to beat the eight-ounce hamburger sandwich. Mix one and half pounds of ground beef and half a pound of ground pork with a teaspoon of salt and a teaspoon of pepper. Divide it into eight parts which you flatten into rounds. Now mix a finely chopped onion with two teaspoons of chili powder, the juice of half a lemon, two slices of bread (soaked and squeezed), half a teaspoon of salt and two tablespoons of butter. Put this mixture in four of the rounds and then cover the others. Press the edges tightly together and barbecue over a medium fire, turning once.

A handful of chopped, fresh mushrooms and a little extra salt and pepper will improve any of these recipes, and leftover cooked rice makes a great substitute for bread. A dab of peanut butter spread on a hamburger before it is barbecued will surprise you and delight the children, and a little peanut butter, mixed well into the meat and spiced with curry powder and lemon juice, is instant exoticism. A little red wine thrown into the frypan after the hamburgers come out will boil down to an instant sauce (so will a little beer), and if you have to impress somebody, hamburger flambées work as well as anything else. I don't know why, but they seem particularly good with rye.

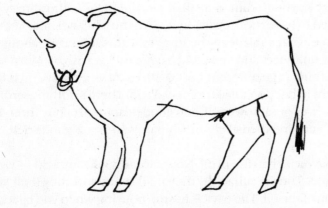

HAMBURGER GREEK-STYLE OR KEFTEDES

1 lb ground beef or lean ground lamb
1 onion, finely chopped
3 - 4 cloves garlic, chopped
a large handful of chopped parsley
a few mint leaves
1 egg
1/2 tsp cinnamon
salt and pepper
2 slices bread, soaked in water and squeezed

Mix all ingredients together and knead it all on a board for a few minutes until soft and pliable. To make it easier to handle, place in the fridge for 1 - 2 hours.

Pinch off lumps as big as walnuts and roll them between your palms. Dust them with flour and fry in hot oil, moving them constantly until they're crisp and brown. Serve in pita bread with a little yoghurt.

HAMBURGER YUGOSLAV-STYLE OR CEVAPCICI

1/2 lb ground pork
1/2 lb ground beef or lamb
1 medium onion, finely chopped
1 tsp paprika
zest of a lemon, very finely chopped
2 slices bread, soaked in water and squeezed
1 clove garlic, chopped
salt

Mix all ingredients together and roll into thumb-sized pieces. Fry them until they're brown all over and serve them with a salad of raw, chopped onion, liberally peppered and splashed with vinegar.

The Greens Of Summer

Fresh salads and your own simple dressings make for marvelous meals.

BASIC SALAD DRESSING

vegetable oil (olive, safflower, sunflower, peanut)
vinegar (or lemon juice, grapefruit juice, orange juice)
1/2 tsp salt
pepper

Half fill an empty spice jar with the oil and carefully add the vinegar until you have approximately three times the amount of oil to vinegar. Add the salt and a good sprinkling of pepper, screw the lid on tight and give it a good shake.

CREAMY EGG DRESSING

Add 1/2 tsp mustard (dry or mixed) and 1 egg yolk to the Basic Salad Dressing and shake again.

FRENCH DRESSING

Add thyme to the Basic Salad Dressing and shake again.

ITALIAN DRESSING

Add oregano to the Basic Salad Dressing and shake again.

The shelves of the supermarkets are heavy on salad dressings this time of year — Italian, French, blue cheese, even curry flavoured. All of them come in nice little bottles, every one of them has a long list of polysyllabic ingredients and each of them, despite the manufacturers' claims, tastes much the same as the others.

Most refrigerators have at least one of these bottles hiding in the dark, back corner, waiting for the annual clearout ("This okay, hon? Better chuck it out, eh?). And often, down in the vegetable compartment, lurks the bottled salad dressing's best friend — the all-purpose, indestructable and anaemic iceberg lettuce, pale, sad and tightly wrapped in Saran wrap, destined to be abandoned on the side of a plate and dumped in the garbage.

Greens are very big these days in gourmet circles. There are fancy vegetables from France and Israel and Thailand, things with names like *mache* and *radicchio* and *puntarella* — all of them indeed wonderful vegetables *if you can find them*.

Most people can't, so they give up and go back to the bottled dressings, the dreary old lettuce and the monster beefsteak, cotton wool-flavoured tomato. The nice local alternatives sit ignored like poor relations at a wedding. So let us found the Society For Simply Super and Sometimes Superbly Simple Salads, make a few dressings and find a few different things to do with them.

The best starting point is a spice jar, the plain and ordinary little jar that used to have the oregano in it, with the label washed off so you can see what's inside. Now forget all this nonsense about teaspoons, millilitres and cups, and half fill the jar with oil. What kind of oil? Anything vegetable, but not 10-30. Extra virgin olive oil is fine if you've got it, but don't make a special trip. There's nothing wrong with sunflower or safflower oil, and good peanut oil (I buy three-litre cans of it very inexpensively in Chinatown) has a good, rich, nutty flavour.

So we have a jar half full of oil. Now carefully add any acid — vinegar, lemon juice. They're all acids, they'll all work and they'll all sink to the bottom of the oil. The trick is to stop pouring when you have about three times as much oil as acid. I say about three because there's nothing critical about it. You may well find that you like equal quantities, and you have control. This business in the jar is creative cooking, even if it doesn't use expensive specialist equipment. Now add a half teaspoon of salt and a good sprinkling of pepper, screw the lid on tight and give it a good shake. That's the basic dressing, smoothed out as efficiently as any blender can do it and ready to use as is or modified. Add a half teaspoon of mustard (dry or mixed) and an egg yolk, shake it again and you have a creamy egg dressing, almost a mayonnaise. Add thyme and you have French dressing, wonderful with either a salad or boiled potatoes. Add oregano for an Italian dressing. Add some finely chopped onion, garlic and a little hot red pepper, and suddenly it's Spanish. Adding soya sauce and sesame seeds, makes a wonderful dressing that transforms plain cold chicken into a Japanese dish. There's no end to the variety you can discover.

Those are the dressings. Now for some salads. When green beans are fresh (skinny, bright green, very crisp and juicy when snapped across), drop them whole into a big pot of boiling, salted water. Boil them furiously for exactly four minutes, drain and immediately rinse with cold running water until they have cooled. Drain again, toss with the basic dressing to which you have added tarragon and you have a French bean salad. A few cubes of gruyère cheese will transform it into a *salade des haricots verts au gruyère*. Add a little feta instead of the gruyere and you have a Greek country salad.

Now use cauliflower, broken into flowerets and rapidly boiled, again for four minutes, drained and tossed with the basic dressing to which this time you have added a half teaspoon of grated nutmeg. That's cauliflower polonaise, which you can eat warm or cold.

For an instant creamy slaw without any of the bother of cooking a dressing, slice a cabbage very thin, make the standard dressing, add an egg, one teaspoon of mustard, some caraway seeds and a little extra salt, then toss it with the cabbage.

Apart from or in addition to the dressing, there are wonderful simple things to add which will transform an ordinary salad into something memorable. There is hardly a restaurant in Canada that doesn't have Caesar salad on its menu. The principal flavouring in a Caesar is anchovies, mash up a couple of fillets and add them to the standard dressing. Suddenly a head of plain lettuce will begin to remind you of that wonderful night you spent at Chez Petunia.

Try the anchovies with the bean salad we started with, and then the cauliflower. Anchovies go with any green vegetable, even coleslaw. They also do wonderful things for potato and beetroot salad, which you might like to try since it looks and tastes spectacular.

Begin by making a jar of standard dressing, then cook a bunch of small beetroots and three or four medium potatoes and hard boil a

SPANISH DRESSING

Add some finely chopped onion, garlic and a little hot pepper flakes or cayenne to the Basic Salad Dressing and shake again.

JAPANESE DRESSING

Add soya sauce and ginger, or soya sauce and sesame seeds to the Basic Salad Dressing and shake again.

FRENCH BEAN SALAD

2 big handfuls of fresh green beans
basic salad dressing with tarragon
gruyère cheese, cubed (optional)

Drop the beans into a large pot of boiling, salted water and boil them furiously for exactly 4 minutes. Drain and rinse with cold running water until cool. Drain again and toss with the dressing. Add cheese if desired.

CAULIFLOWER POLONAISE

1 cauliflower, broken into florets
basic dressing with 1/2 tsp grated nutmeg

Boil the cauliflower as above for exactly 4 minutes again. Drain and toss with the dressing. Serve hot or cold.

CREAMY COLESLAW

1 cabbage, very finely sliced
basic dressing with these additions:
1 egg
1 tsp mustard
caraway seeds
salt

Toss the cabbage and dressing together and serve.

POTATO AND BEETROOT SALAD

a bunch of small beetroots, cooked
3 - 4 medium potatoes, cooked
2 hard-boiled eggs
1 medium onion, finely chopped
1 can anchovy fillets
parsley, chopped
basic dressing

Thinly slice the beetroots. Halve the potatoes and slice them a little thicker. Mash the eggs and set aside.

Arrange the potato slices around the edge of a shallow bowl. Make a second and maybe a third ring. Arrange the beetroot slices in the middle.

Fry the onion over medium heat using the basic dressing instead of oil. Add the anchovies and stir until they melt. Pour this mixture over the beetroots and potatoes and sprinkle with the egg and parsley. Serve warm or cold.

TOMATO AND OLIVE OIL SALAD

3 or 4 ripe tomatoes
salt
oregano
olive oil

Slice the tomatoes, arrange them slightly overlapping on a plate. Sprinkle with salt and oregano. Drizzle good olive oil over the top and allow to sit at room temperature for 1 - 2 hours. Serve with plenty of fresh bread (no butter).

couple of eggs. Peel and thinly slice the beetroot. Slice the potatoes a bit thicker and cut the slices into halves. Mash the eggs with a fork and set them aside. Now the fancy bit. Arrange the potato slices around the edge of a shallow soup plate bowl. Then make a second ring, and maybe a third, one inside the other. Arrange the beetroot slices in the middle.

Finely chop a medium onion and cook it over medium heat in a frypan, using the standard dressing instead of oil. Add a can of anchovy fillets as soon as the pan gets warm and mash them around until they melt. Now pour the whole mixture over the beetroots and potatoes. Mix a little chopped parsley in with the mashed egg and sprinkle it over the beets. Eat it warm or cold. This potato salad, with the traditional mayonnaise, is also much safer to take on picnics.

The Italians make almost anything into a salad which they call *verdura*. Asparagus, broad beans, little fresh peas, beet tops — whatever ingredients they choose, they just quickly cook and cool them, add the standard dressing and keep them for lunch.

Tomatoes have sufficient acid in them not to need extra. So just slice them, arrange them slightly overlapping on a plate and sprinkle with salt and oregano. Then drizzle the best olive oil you can find over the top. Leave them at room temperature for an hour or two, and then eat them with fresh bread. Don't use butter, because you will discover the joy and wonderful taste of sopping up the olive oil/tomato/oregano juice.

And don't forget that those bright orange calendula petals are edible. Just a few of them sprinkled over a salad make it look wonderful. Daisy petals, nasturtium leaves are also edible. A little bottle of standard dressing will open all kinds of doors.

Garlic –
The Pungent Poltergeist

Steven Spielberg has seen to it that ghosts don't scare us anymore. Today's little kids yawn at horror stories, vampires belong strictly to the black-and-white late, late nighters and strange noises downstairs are more likely to be the fridge on the blink than a poltergeist on the rampage. We just don't scare as easily as we used to, not unless there's a $12-million special-effects budget and a big publicity campaign telling us in advance that we're going to need seatbelts not to be freaked right out of our seats.

But there is one word we all know which never fails to frighten at least half the people sitting talking around a table. You don't even have to say it aloud — just thinking about it is enough for the vibrations to start, and even the most sophisticated friends will suddenly wish they were back in Sheepdip, Alberta, where kids could grow up, marry and become grandparents without ever having to accept the presence of, or even know about, *garlic.*

Almost everybody has a horror story about garlic, and those who don't will quickly dream one up. Social lives are ruined and engagements broken ("And then she had supper with his family . . ."). Everybody knows that the Royal Family *never* eats garlic (although there are rumours that it's the real problem between Chuck and Di), and I'm quite sure that one day there will be a sad story in the newspaper about a kid refused entry to grade one because of garlic. He finishes up starving and illiterate on Skid Row where a kind social worker discovers, just before he fades away, that he has an I.Q. of 220 and could easily have developed a cure for nuclear warfare and the common cold if only society had tolerated his addiction. And everybody knows what makes pit bulls mean, right?

So it won't be long before *Garlic, The Movie* is made. "First the silent movies, then the talkies, and now . . . Garth Drabinsky brings you *the smellies. . . .*" T-shirts, deodorants and a complete line of garlic-flavoured greeting cards, all released simultaneously with an exposure of corruption in high places. But unlike *Jaws* or *The Birds,* which scared people out of bathtubs and even gave budgie birds a bad name, *Garlic* will develop a cult following bigger than Madonna's

AÏOLI

4 cloves of garlic, peeled
2 egg yolks
1/2 tsp salt
1/2 tsp pepper
1 tsp dry mustard
juice of half a lemon
1 cup oil

Put the cloves in a blender or food processor and give them a quick whiz. Add the egg yolks, salt and pepper, mustard and lemon juice and blend until smooth. With the machine running slowly drizzle in the oil until the mayonnaise thickens and becomes cream coloured. Add 1 tsp warm water or some lemon juice if it becomes too thick and whiz a few seconds more.

and bring all the secret garlic addicts out of their closets and into the streets.

Ever since cooking began garlic has been the victim of bad press. Nobody would come to terms with it, except as a cure. Bad colds, rheumatism, unsatisfactory love lives — anything wrong with you could be put right with a discreet, *medicinal* application of garlic. But garlic for itself, for pure pleasure, for a nice, big, round taste, for unique and indefinable *satisfaction?* That was something we had a hard time accepting, and all kinds of recipes were developed which involved wearing rubber gloves, buying expensive garlic presses or, in the most chic of gourmet circles, whispering over the salad bowl, as reverently as an FM announcer, "Garlic!"

Most of these recipes are nonsense. Timidity has nothing to do with cooking, particularly when you're dealing with garlic. Let's begin with *aïoli,* the garlic mayonnaise which will transform a simple piece of fish, cold chicken or even just plain boiled potatoes into a *dish* — something for your tongue and all your other senses to reflect upon while your teeth slowly and contemplatively chew it.

Aïoli, like all truly wonderful things, is easy to make. It will keep for three days in the refrigerator and it will bring you to a basic understanding of how to handle garlic without being scared.

First squash four cloves of garlic on a board, one at a time, using a broad-bladed knife or the heel of your hand. Just squash them enough to pop the skins and the meat will shake out. If you really worry about the smell on your fingers, run your hands under cold water — *not hot.* Cold water will wash the aromatic oil off your skin, while hot water will open your pores and let it in, to emerge later through all your other pores.

Now put the garlic cloves into the blender or food processor. Give them a quick whizz, add two egg yolks, a half teaspoon of salt, a half teaspoon of pepper, one teaspoon of dry mustard and the juice of half a lemon. Blend it until it's smooth, and with the machine still running drizzle in one cup of peanut, safflower or inexpensive olive oil (this is neither the time nor the place for extra-virgin). The drizzling must be slow — a thin and continuous stream — and then the mayonnaise (that's all it is, just a garlic mayonnaise called aïoli) will thicken and become very light cream coloured. If it gets too thick (listen to the motor wishing it could shift gears), add a teaspoon of warm water or more lemon juice and whizz it a few seconds longer.

That's all there is to it. Now you have about two cups of aïoli ready to brighten up a salad, fish or meat, to spread of bread, to use as a dip for vegetables or, simplest of all, to mix with a handful of chopped parsley and slather liberally over potatoes, old or new, or thick slices of fresh garden tomatoes. Mashed potatoes can be made dramatically different by using two or three tablespoons of aïoli instead of butter (don't add milk, and use a bit more salt to taste). The French make a fish soup which they call *bourride*. You can do almost the same thing by stirring a teaspoon of aïoli into an otherwise anaemic bowl of clam chowder and sprinkling a little red pepper over it.

Having arrived at this point of casual intimacy with garlic, we will now disclose the big secret — you don't really have to peel garlic at all.

Garlic fried chicken is basically Spanish, a simple and super dish, good hot or cold for dinner parties or picnics, to take on the boat or to a ball game. But before we begin, a few words on pan-frying, particularly on the pan-frying of chicken, which tends to stick: just remember not to put the oil in the pan and then heat it up. Rather, heat the pan dry and add the oil later. Let the oil get hot enough to cook with, then add the chicken. For some inexplicable reason it won't stick if you do it this way.

So you have two tablespoons of oil in a hot pan. Add six or eight pieces of chicken, skin side down. Don't overcrowd them. Let the undersides fry about five minutes without moving them about or peeking (the second most frequent cause of sticking).

Meanwhile, separate about three heads of garlic into cloves, which should give you around 40 or 50 cloves, all still in their white skins. Turn the chicken over and place the unpeeled cloves in the spaces between the pieces. After another five minutes shove the garlic cloves under the chicken, put the lid on and cook for half an hour over medium heat, again without peeking.

When the lid comes off there will be an instant explosion of juicy, warm perfume which says somebody's grandma lives here. Sprinkle furiously with freshly ground pepper and squeeze a lot of lemon juice over it all. Eat it with bread, or over rice, or with boiled potatoes. Make sure each person has a share of the garlic cloves, which have shrivelled and gone dark in their skins. Take the cloves one at a time and squeeze them like toothpaste onto bread or into your mouth. They won't taste like garlic at all, but like chestnuts, round and smooth and rich. And you'll never be scared again.

GARLIC FRIED CHICKEN

6 - 8 pieces chicken
2 tbsp oil
40 - 50 cloves garlic, unpeeled
lemon juice
fresh ground pepper

Heat the oil in a pan and add the chicken, skin side down. Fry about 5 minutes without moving them. Turn the chicken over and add the unpeeled garlic cloves. After 5 minutes move the garlic cloves under the chicken, put the lid on and cook for half an hour over medium heat.

When cooked, remove the lid and sprinkle liberally with freshly ground pepper and lots of lemon juice. Serve with bread, rice or potatoes.

Immodest But Honest Eating

FRIED CHICKEN

chicken legs, wings, breasts

BATTER

1 egg
1/2 cup milk
1 cup flour
1/2 tsp salt
1/4 cup yellow cornmeal
1/2 tsp baking powder
dash pepper
dash paprika

SAUCE

1/2 can peaches
juice of a lemon
1/2 cup water
3 tbsp brown sugar
1 tbsp butter
1 tbsp vinegar
1/2 tsp paprika
salt
cayenne pepper

In a bowl combine the egg and milk. In another bowl combine the flour, salt, cornmeal, baking powder, pepper and paprika. Dip the chicken first in the egg, then the flour mixture and deep fry until golden.

Meanwhile make the sauce combining all the above ingredients and heat until thick. Serve with the chicken.

One not-too-distant day it will appear on the television screens and the supermarket shelves, in the papers and the magazines, anywhere that a million dollars can buy advertising. And a million can-opening cooks will buy it and, like all can-opening cooks, be disappointed without knowing why.

"Soul," it will be called. "Just add a pinch to everything." There will be a picture of a smiling lady, and some smiling children, and perhaps a smiling man. Probably with Colonel Whatsit beaming from a background of smiling black faces.

This recipe came to me from a smiling black face in the middle of New York. But she was careful to point out that soul isn't the monopoly of any colour or race and it doesn't come out of a bottle or packet. "It's sharing what there is with who there is." Princess Pamela has since written a cookbook but long before that, when I was cold and had no money, she fed me fried chicken, gave me wine and told me the recipe.

She had a little restaurant that seated 16. And she cooked in a kitchen the size of a broom closet, without fancy pots or thermostats — not even a fan. She measured things with the palm of her hand — a little palmful was a teaspoon, a big one a tablespoon. She fried in a big old pan with two or three inches of oil in it, and she always had the plates hot . . . .

You can cook this fried chicken on a two-burner hotplate with one saucepan — make the sauce first, then wipe it out and make the chicken. Strain the oil when it's cold, through an old nylon stocking, and put it in a jar ready for the next time around.

In a bowl combine one egg and half a cup of milk. In another bowl combine one cup of flour, half a teaspoon of salt, a quarter-cup of yellow cornmeal, half a teaspoon of baking powder and a dash each of pepper and paprika. Dip chicken first in egg, then in flour mixture, then deep fry until golden. Meanwhile make a sauce of a half-can of peaches, the juice of one lemon, half a cup of water, three tablespoons of brown sugar, one tablespoon of butter, one tablespoon of vinegar, half a teaspoon of paprika and salt and cayenne pepper to taste. Heat the sauce until thick and serve with chicken.

Wolves, beautiful women in horse-drawn sleighs, ice and snow everywhere and potatoes and vodka. You know what Russia is like. A primitive version of North Dakota.

It was quite a shock to find that there are light, joyous, sunny dishes in Russia, food made as exciting as any Italian ever imagined — all of them easy to make and most of them digestible, even without vodka.

I was shown this dish using pomegranate juice; which is hard to get. Red wine is a perfectly acceptable substitute, or you can use cranberry juice with an extra clove of garlic and a teaspoonful of vinegar, or plain grape juice with a little vinegar and some orange peel. Don't get bogged down in dogma; just enjoy this thick, dark red, flavourful dish. If you have sauce left over, keep it in a cup in the fridge and use it on spaghetti.

Cut chicken breasts or thighs into bite-sized pieces and fry them over medium heat in two tablespoons of oil for two minutes. Meanwhile chop a medium onion, cut up two medium tomatoes and chop very fine two tablespoons of walnuts and two cloves of garlic. Add onions and garlic to the chicken, stirring constantly for one minute, then add tomatoes, walnuts, one teaspoon of salt, half a teaspoon of cayenne and one glass of red wine, stirring between each addition. Cover and cook 15 minutes over medium heat, stirring once or twice. Cut up broccoli into flowers (or use frozen peas). Put the vegetables on the chicken, sprinkle with a half-teaspoon of salt and the juice of half a lemon. Cover and cook five minutes.

This is a simple fall soup, a special for someone you specially want to please. Tomatoes are cheap in the fall, and it is not really a very expensive soup, but is almost obscenely luxurious, a smooth, soft, gentle, fattening, rich thing which makes a very pleasant light supper, particularly by the fire and with, if you can find it, a bottle of that Portuguese green wine, very cold.

The important thing is not to boil it, or it will curdle. Gentle it all the way through, gentle in the butter in slivers, stirring all the time, and gentle in the cream, stirring all the time. It should be a pleasant, soft sensation, and once you have started adding things, keep the heat soft and gentle. If you let it boil it will curdle, so be nice to it.

Croutons are just cubes of oldish bread, warmed, rather than fried, very slowly in lots of butter. I usually do them in the oven in my big iron frying pan. Melt the butter, toss the cubes in it until they are coated, add a chopped clove of garlic if you wish or a couple of handfuls of chopped parsley and put them in a low oven (250°F) for an hour or so. Let them cool, and keep in a screw-top jar to use in soups and salads, or just eat them with a glass of wine while you wait for dinner to cook.

And don't forget the dill. If you haven't got any, get some and start using it on all sorts of things. Cook beets in it, sprinkle it on fish, especially shellfish, and even if you have to finish up one day with a

CHICKEN TOVARICH

chicken breasts or thighs for 6
2 tbsp oil
1 medium onion, chopped
2 medium tomatoes, chopped
2 tbsp walnuts, finely chopped
2 cloves garlic, finely chopped
1 1/2 tsp salt
1/2 tsp cayenne pepper
1 glass red wine
bunch of broccoli, cut into florets (or use frozen peas)
juice of half a lemon

Cut the chicken into bite-sized pieces and fry over medium heat in the oil for 2 minutes. Add onion and garlic and stir for 1 minute. Add tomatoes, walnuts, salt, cayenne pepper and red wine, stirring constantly. Cover and cook for 15 minutes over medium heat. Add broccoli to the chicken, sprinkle with 1/2 tsp salt and the lemon juice. Cover and cook for 5 minutes.

TOMATO AND DILL SOUP

8 large, ripe tomatoes
2 cups water
1 tbsp sugar
a pinch of salt
1 tsp dill
4 oz butter
1 pt whipping cream
black pepper
parsley, chopped

Plunge the tomatoes into boiling water for 30 seconds and peel. Add the water, sugar, salt and dill and simmer, covered for 45 minutes. Strain the soup and return to pot over low heat. Add the butter in small slivers. Do not boil. Take off heat and add the whipping cream gradually, stirring until smooth. Reheat, but do not boil. Serve hot with black pepper, parsley and croutons.

can of soup, throw in a little dill and surprise yourself. Canned tomato soup with dill in it tastes almost as good as the advertisements say it does.

Drop eight large ripe tomatoes in boiling water for 30 seconds and peel. Add two cups of water, one tablespoon of sugar, a pinch of salt and one teaspoon of dill. Simmer, covered, 45 minutes. Strain soup and return to pot over low heat, adding four ounces of butter in small slivers. Do not boil. Take off heat and add one pint of whipping cream gradually, stirring until smooth. Reheat, but do not boil. Serve hot with black pepper and chopped parsley and croutons.

A Litany of Comfort

Recipes to hold the damp
and dreary winter at bay.

Winter will be scratching at the back door one of these mornings, sad and cold, damp and dreary — not at all like the glamorous winter of the picture postcards, smart and crisp in brand-new snow with holly in its hair, robins sitting on the phone lines and logs crackling in the fireplace.

Early winter is comfort time — hot chocolate, back rubs, oatmeal for breakfast and Sunday morning bubble baths. It's a great time for comforting cooking, the easy, slow, fragrant cooking of soups and stews, casseroles and hot pots which turn even the smallest house into a warm and welcoming place to come home to.

Leeks are plentiful in late fall, potatoes still fresh and onions at their best. Leek and potato soup is the cheapest, simplest and easiest of all soups to make, the sort of thing that even dedicated can openers can make. But most of all, it's comforting.

You need two potatoes, unpeeled and diced, one bunch of leeks (two or three, depending on their size) halved lengthwise and then sliced across and a finely chopped medium onion. The textbooks tell you to discard the green part of the leek, but ignore them — the green part is where the flavour and colour come from. Certainly you should throw away the tired looking outside leaves and anything obviously ancient, but the rest — carefully washed, because leeks collect a lot of sand — you slice thinly and use.

Heat two tablespoons of oil in a big saucepan and stir in the onion for two minutes. Add the leeks and stir another two minutes. Then add the potatoes and stir yet another two minutes, until everything glistens. Add a half-teaspoon each of ground pepper and salt and enough hot water from the tap to cover it all by the thickness of your finger. Simmer for 30 minutes, stirring occasionally, and add half a teaspoon of ground nutmeg. This is the time to warm the plates and cut some thick slices of good bread. Then add about half a litre of milk or coffee cream, or half a cup of heavy cream, stir well and serve immediately.

If you want the dish to be elegant, run the soup through a food processor or blender before adding the cream. For even more

LEEK AND POTATO SOUP

2 potatoes, unpeeled and diced
2 - 3 leeks, halved lengthwise and thinly sliced
1 medium onion, finely chopped
2 tbsp oil
1/2 litre milk or coffee cream, or 1/2 cup heavy cream
1/2 tsp salt
1/2 tsp pepper
1/2 tsp ground nutmeg

Heat the oil and stir in the onion for two minutes. Add the leeks and stir another 2 minutes. Add the potatoes, stir again. Add the pepper, salt, nutmeg and enough hot water to cover it all. Simmer 30 minutes, stirring occasionally. Add the milk or cream, stir well and serve immediately.

For elegance, put the soup through a blender or processor before adding the cream.

CABBAGE AND GARLIC SAUSAGE STEW

1 fresh green cabbage
1 garlic sausage or Ukrainian sausage
2 tbsp butter
1 bottle beer
caraway seeds
1 tsp ground pepper

Cut the sausage into bite sized chunks and the cabbage into thick slices. Melt butter and toss the cabbage for two minutes. Sprinkle with the pepper. Add the sausage, stir well and pour in half a bottle of beer.

Simmer, lid on, for two minutes, sprinkle generously with caraway seeds, stir and serve with fresh bread.

elegance, process it really smooth and serve it cold, telling people it's a *potage parmentier.*

You can make a big pot and freeze it in small containers, and instead of using oil you can fry a few slices of chopped bacon until the fat runs out. Or add a bit of ham, or use chicken stock instead of water, or even better, finely chop a bunch of kale and add it just after adding the potatoes. Then you'll have a Portuguese soup called *caldo verde.* The more stuff you add, the more seasonings you'll need, but don't add salt until the very end, just before the cream.

Now let's think about a stew. Not the usual long-term, preplanned stew, but a really fast, 20-minute wonder which is good enough to serve to company. The only exotic item you'll need is a package of caraway seeds, available in any supermarket. You will also need a garlic sausage or a Ukranian sausage, or even, if you're desperate, plain old smoky wieners. Then get out a plump, fresh, shiny-on-the-outside green cabbage, two tablespoons of butter, a bottle of beer and the caraway seeds.

Cut the meat into bite sized chunks (big bites) and the cabbage into slices as thick as the *TV Guide.* Melt the butter in a big saucepan or deep pan and toss the cabbage in it for two minutes. Sprinkle with a good sized teaspoon of pepper (remember, this is a winter food). Add the smoked meat, stir it well and add a half-bottle of beer. Simmer with lid on tight for two minutes, sprinkle very generously with caraway seeds (fenel or anise will do, but caraway is the best), stir and serve with lots of good bread and more beer. If you don't want to use beer, use apple juice. This is basically a German dish that I came across in a logging camp up north, where it was the most popular item on the weekly menu.

Then there's mushroom and potato stew, which the French, who make it at this time of year, call *ragoût de champignons.* They eat it as a main course for supper or as a big, hearty, vegetable dish which will stretch a smallish chicken into a meal for six.

Once again, it's ridiculously easy. You'll need two large, unpeeled, cubed potatoes, three cloves of crushed garlic, one small can of anchovies and a big bag of fresh whole mushrooms. You will also need thyme and pepper, and most of all you will need to learn not to be scared of the anchovies when you discover that they melt and become part of the sauce, which doesn't taste at all like anchovies and is smooth and velvety.

Heat two tablespoons of oil in a big saucepan and fry the potato cubes until they just change colour and are about half cooked. Add the anchovies, oil and all, and the garlic. Stir well until the anchovies have melted, then add the mushrooms and turn everything together. Sprinkle with pepper and a teaspoon of thyme, put the lid on tight, turn the heat to low and let it cook for 20 minutes, stirring once or twice. The juices from the mushrooms will come out and mingle with the starch from the potatoes, the anchovies will bind them together and you will finish up with a big, flavourful dish which will look even nicer if you sprinkle it with chopped parsley. Leftovers, whizzed through the blender and heated with a little milk or cream, will make a wonderful soup.

And finally, in this litany of comfort, a recipe for steamed pudding, which takes exactly 20 minutes to make and cook. It will use up all those berries which you so carefully froze in the long-forgotten summer, and if you didn't manage *that* it works equally well with any frozen fruit. First you make a pudding dough: one cup of flour, a half-teaspoon of salt, two teaspoons of baking powder and a couple of tablespoons of sugar. Stir in one or two eggs (two make it richer) and a half-cup of milk. This should produce a lumpy dough. Now place one pound of berries frozen or canned) in the bottom of a deep saucepan and sprinkle them with a little sugar. Spoon the flour mixture on top of everything. Don't push down or mix; just leave it. Put the lid on and simmer for 17 to 20 minutes. Serve it directly from the pan with a big spoon which can dig down and scoop out the fruit and the juices, which haven't soaked into the pudding. If you want to be fancy put a little booze, the finely chopped peel of a lemon or a little honey in with the fruit. If you haven't got berries, apples will happily substitute, but with them you'll need brown sugar and a little water to make a syrup — and maybe some cinnamon for taste. And in a pinch you can use three tablespoons of jam mixed with half a cup of water. Everybody loves a pudding maker.

MUSHROOM AND POTATO STEW

3 - 4 potatoes
2 tbsp oil
1/2 lb mushrooms
2 cloves garlic, roughly chopped
4 anchovy fillets
1/2 tsp salt
1/2 tsp pepper
1/2 tsp dried thyme or oregano

Cube the potatoes. Heat the oil in a heavy saucepan and toss the potatoes in it until they start to change color. Add the garlic and the anchovies and stir until the anchovies melt. Add the mushrooms whole if small, halved if larger and the seasonings. Toss everything together, put the lid on and cook for 15 minutes stirring occasionally.

For an additional delicacy add some dried orange peel along with the anchovies and garlic.

STEAMED PUDDING

1 cup flour
1/2 tsp salt
2 tsp baking powder
2 tbsp sugar
1 or 2 eggs
1/2 cup milk
1 lb berries (fresh or frozen)

Mix together the flour, salt, baking powder and sugar. Stir in the eggs and milk to produce a lumpy dough. Place the berries in the bottom of a deep saucepan and sprinkle with a little sugar. Spoon the flour mixture on top, put the lid on and simmer for 17 - 20 minutes. Serve directly from the pan. For an extra touch, you can add some booze to the berries, or the chopped peel of a lemon or a little honey.

What's In a Name?

Everything, when you're talking about stew.
If you want people to eat it,
give it another name.

BEEF, ORANGE AND ANISEED STEW

1 lb stewing beef, cubed
3 tbsp flour
2 tbsp oil
2 large, ripe tomatoes, chopped (or a can)
3 tbsp soya sauce
1 tsp aniseed
1 tsp dry mustard
1/2 tsp ground pepper
peel of an orange
2 anchovy fillets (optional)

Toss the beef in a bag with the flour. Fry over medium heat in oil until all sides are lightly browned. Add the pepper, soya sauce, aniseed, mustard, anchovies (if using), tomatoes and the orange peel. Simmer, covered, for 1 1/2 - 2 hours.

For serving on special occasions, get a large pumpkin, cut the top off, place in a saucepan and scoop out the seeds. After the stew has cooked for 90 minutes, spoon it into the pumpkin, replace the top and put it all in the oven at 400°F for half an hour. Bring to the table, and serve the stew from the pumpkin scooping out chunks of pumpkin as you go.

Wintertime is stew time. And stew time is a great time for those honestly lazy cooks, people who want not just to *feed* their families and friends, but to *fill* them and still have a bit left over for dinner the next day. Above all, nobody who is honestly lazy wants too many dishes to wash.

Stews are the obvious choice. But there are two problems — children and friends. Most children know from the time they're born that eating stew is not just socially unacceptable, it's also *morally wrong.* It's only slightly worse than wearing runners with seven eyelets when eight are in fashion, and almost as bad as eating liver, something they are forced to do.

Then come your friends, who manage something less than their usual delighted smiles when, right after you've gotten their coats off and they go into their usual "something sure smells good" routine, you tell them "stew." It's not your shame, it's theirs. They feel inadequate — not quite good enough, almost second class, and they think it's because of the terrible bottle of wine they brought last time or the Christmas card they didn't send you last year. They think that stew is your revenge, and that next morning in the gossip column of the local paper their names will appear: "Mr. and Mrs. Jones were entertained last night at the Robinsons. They were given *stew*...."

Neither of these problems is really yours. But the solution is. The best food in the world comes out of a stew pot. French, Greek, Italian or African — the origin doesn't matter, because all stews have the same, magic ingredients of care and time. Any fool can burn a steak or fry a hamburger, but stew, while it doesn't call for any great intellectual triumphs, is a product of love and stability. Stew is security. So while the house develops warmth and richness that comes from a slowly simmering pot, you and everybody else, including the cat, gently relax into certain knowledge that right where you are is the best possible place to be in the world — warm and kind and loving, like a great, generous, garlic flavoured backrub.

They will sense this, the friends and the kids both, but they'll still have suspicion lingering in the unswept corners of their minds. So you must call it something else — a *ragoût* or a *mireton,* a *daube* or a *grillade,* all perfectly respectable words for stew even if you can't pronounce them. If you're imaginative you will invent a story to go with it: "This is Michael Jackson's favourite supper. His mother airfreights it to him on tour . . . ." Or if you can find a couple of appropriately foreign postcards you can deceive your friends into believing the story of the time you were staying with the sultan of Swat: "It's a ceremonial dish they make for special occasions. They call it *rumiani . . . .*"

Whatever you do, a stew is a stew and the procedure is invariably the same, even if the ingredients are different. Beef, pork, lamb or chicken stews need long, slow cooking, while fish and vegetable stews never take more than half an hour. The only important thing about being a good stew cook is knowing the secret ingredient to use to make it into something unusual and special.

Take this beef stew, which is an adaptation of something I once ate in Naples. There are two special ingredients in it, both easily available and inexpensive. Toss one pound of cubed stewing beef in a bag with three tablespoons of flour. Fry over medium heat in two tablespoons of oil until all sides are lightly browned. Add, all at once, a half-teaspoon of ground pepper, three tablespoons of soya sauce, one teaspoon of aniseed, one teaspoon of dry mustard, three large, ripe chopped tomatoes (or a can) and the peel of an orange. Simmer covered for one and a half to two hours. The orange and the aniseed give the stew a richness much like a northern Chinese stir-fry, but while everybody likes it, nobody can identify the special ingredients. You just smile.

To make it even more Italian, add a couple of anchovy fillets at the same time as the seasonings. If you want to make it a show stopper, get a pumpkin a bit bigger than your head, cut the top off, put it in a saucepan or casserole that comes half-way up its sides and scoop out the seeds. After the stew has cooked for 90 minutes, spoon it into the pumpkin, replace the top and put the whole thing into a 400°F oven for half an hour. Bring it to the table and serve the stew directly from the pumpkin, scooping out chunks of pumpkin as you go. I call it Mrs. Marco Polo's Homecoming For Her Long-Lost Son. You can call it whatever you like.

Beer is another ingredient which transforms the simple and ordinary into a reputation-making dish. ("Why don't you ask my mother how *she* made a beef stew?) This stew develops a lovely dense, rich brown, velvety sauce. The Belgians call it *carbonades de boeuf à la flamande.* I call it six-pack stew. It takes two pans to start with, but one soaks clean while the other cooks.

Once again, start by frying cubed and floured beef in a little oil until the outsides are brown. Remove the meat and set it aside. Meanwhile,

SIX-PACK STEW OR BOEUF CARBONADE

1 lb stewing beef, cubed
5 tbsp flour
2 large onions, thinly sliced
2 tbsp oil
1 tbsp butter
1 1/2 bottles beer
2 cloves garlic, chopped
1 bay leaf
1 tsp dried thyme
1/2 tsp dried basil
1 eggcup vinegar
a good sprinkle of pepper
salt (or 2 anchovy fillets)

Toss the beef in a bag with 3 tbsp flour. Fry in oil until all sides are lightly browned. Meanwhile, in another pan, fry the onions in butter very slowly and stirring constantly. Add 2 tbsp flour to the <u>meat</u> pan and cook over medium heat, stirring vigorously until light brown. Add the beer, garlic, bay leaf, thyme, basil, vinegar, pepper and salt. Stir well.

Layer the onions and meat in a casserole and bake in a 250° - 275°F oven for 3 hours. Serve over a bed of egg noodles or with plain, boiled potatoes.

PORK CHOP AND APPLE STEW

4 pork chops
1 medium onion, thinly sliced
2 apples, cored and sliced
crosswise
oil
cinnamon
1 cup apple juice or cider
1 bay leaf
1 tsp salt
1 tsp dried basil or thyme
cheese

Brown the chops quickly over high heat in a little oil. Add the onion and fry over medium heat. Remove the meat and onions from the pan and keep warm. Add some more oil and fry the apples until they're light brown. Dust with cinnamon. Layer the apples, meat and onions in a casserole, baking dish or frypan. Add the apple juice or cider, bay leaf, salt and basil or thyme. Bake for 45 minutes with the lid on tight. Then cover with cheese and broil until brown and bubbly.

in the other pan, fry two large, thinly sliced onions in a little butter. This frying is important; it has to be done very slowly over low heat and the onions must be stirred a lot so the natural sugar develops. Now add two tablespoons of flour to the *meat* pan and cook over medium heat, stirring vigorously until light brown. This is the sauce base, to which you now add one and a half bottles of beer (any kind of beer will do but dark is best), two chopped cloves of garlic, one bay leaf, one teaspoon of dried basil. Throw in an eggcup of vinegar, a generous sprinkle of ground pepper and some salt (or a couple of anchovy fillets). Stir well and you have the sauce. Layer the onions and meat in a casserole, cover with the sauce and bake in a slow oven (250° to 275°F) for three hours while you go shopping, or to a movie, or to the hairdresser. The finished product will be thick and rich, perfect for serving over a bed of egg noodles or with a big dish of plain, boiled potatoes.

Pork, which is usually cheap in the winter, is used in a lot of European stews, particularly where apples are grown. This is an especially quick and easy stew which is fancy enough for company, simple enough for family and can be made in less than an hour in a deep frypan. I use chops because they're easy to serve. (I always have half a dozen chops in the freezer, which I separate with waxed paper before freezing so that they don't stick together). They can be fried without defrosting for this dish. You can also use pork butt or shoulder and cut it into cubes yourself so you won't be paying almost twice as much for pork stew.

So, chops or cubes are browned quickly over high heat in a little oil. Now fry a medium, thinly sliced onion in the same pan over medium heat. Next, move everything out of the pan onto a plate, add a little more oil and fry two apples, cored and sliced crosswise, until they are light brown. Dust with cinnamon. Layer the apples, meat and onions in a casserole, baking dish or deep frypan. Add one cup of apple juice or cider, a bay leaf and one teaspoon each of salt and dry basil or thyme. Bake for 45 minutes with lid on tight. Then cover with cheese and broil until it's brown and bubbly.

Cider, apple juice, beer, orange peel, apples — try making stews with anything that's cheap and in season. Just one final word of advice: if you include mushrooms in your stew, add them last and leave them in for no more that 15 minutes.

Cabbage – The Closet Vegetable

Cabbage in season is bright and shiny, heavy as a bowling ball and cheap. But like rutabagas, it seems to sit on the produce shelves of the supermarkets, unloved, unwanted and, worst of all, *ignored.*

Cabbage suffers from radical discrimination. Generations of Brits remember (vigorously, though they deny it) cabbage boiled into smelly, tasteless pulp and served, sodden with its pale grey juices, as an essential part of dinner every night from Tuesday clear through to Sunday.

On Mondays, if they were lucky and not too well off, they were served cabbage in a dish called bubble and squeak. If they were extremely unlucky, and blessed with parents who believed in health as a sort of punishment to be endured ("Of course it tastes nasty — that's why it's good for you!"), they were forced to drink this cabbage water cold. It looked like the puddle in the driveway where the transmission leaked oil, and tasted no better.

To second- and third-generation Europeans, cabbage evokes memories and flavours of poverty. Family albums have browning, dog-eared photographs of Grandma in ringlets surrounded by *kulaks* and cabbages, and there are stories of old-country Christmases: "There was no turkey; we ate cabbage stuffed with cabbage. And toys? Cabbages too . . . ."

There is no Miss Cabbage in the annual parade of beauty queens, and no cabbage capital of the world. Cabbage gets very little and usually very bad press. Once a year recipes for cabbage rolls appear in the newspapers, and coleslaw gets its turn at the beginning of summer — usually as part of the list of things that can cause food poisoning if you're not careful on a picnic. But full-page spreads with colour photography? No. "Mayor proclaims November Cabbage Month"? No. Cabbage is a closet vegetable — people must be eating it out there, but nobody wants to own up to it.

Among the tunafish casseroles and brown-rice stodges of PTA potluck suppers there will sometimes, with a little luck, be hiding a dish of homemade *holupchi* which you should point out to nobody

CABBAGE AND PORK SAUSAGE

1 4-lb cabbage
1 1/2 lb best pork sausage
salt and pepper
butter

Slit the sausages and crumble the meat. Slice the cabbage crosswise and drop into boiling, salted water for exactly 3 minutes. Run under cold water, drain well and remove hard centre core.

Butter a pot and layer about one-third of the cabbage in the bottom. Salt lightly, and pepper generously. Put about half of the meat over the cabbage, cover it with another third of the cabbage. Repeat the salt and pepper. Add the remainder of the meat and the last third of cabbage and some more salt and pepper. Dot with butter, cover tightly and either bake at 300°F or simmer gently on the stove for 3 hours. Cut into wedges and serve.

and immediately, quietly, secretly and completely devour. If it is an exceptionally large dish you may have to rearrange a flower vase to hide it while you take a few breaths between mouthfuls.

But we're not going to rerun the cabbage rolls, which require a little too much work and practice to ensure that they don't fall apart. Far better that we start with the *simplest* cabbage dish I know — a one-pot dish which has three ingredients plus a little salt and pepper and is good enough (sophisticated seems the wrong word to apply to cabbage) for company. You can cook it in the oven or on top of the stove, and it reheats well, although I have enjoyed a slab of it cold after getting home at three in the morning. It's a French peasant dish — and in France the nicest thing you can call your best beloved is *mon petit chou* (my little cabbage).

Start with a cabbage of about two kilograms (four pounds) and about 750 grams (one and a half pounds) of the very best pork sausage you can buy. Those are the two main ingredients, and you'll also need a lump of butter about as big as an egg. The cabbage can be a firm, green one, a crinkly-leafed savoy or even a Chinese cabbage (*choy sam*), but the sausage must be real sausage from a butcher and most certainly *not* anything of the prebrowned, reheat-and-serve variety.

Slit the sausages, giving the skins to the cat, and crumble the meat. Slice the cabbage crosswise and drop it into boiling, salted water for exactly three minutes. Run it under cold water to stop the cooking process, drain it well and remove the hard centre core. Butter a pot and layer about one-third of the cabbage over the bottom. Salt lightly and pepper generously. Place about half of the crumbled sausage meat over the cabbage, cover it with another third of the cabbage, salt and pepper it again, add the rest of the sausage meat and finish with the remainder of the cabbage and a little more salt and pepper. Dot with butter, cover tightly and either bake at 350°F or simmer very gently on top of the stove for three hours. Chinese cabbage will take about two hours and savoy about two and a half.

Cut into wedges and serve, preferably on a cold winter's night, with beer or cheap Hungarian red wine — cheap enough to stain your teeth. If you want to show off, two dozen peeled chestnuts sliced in with the sausage meat would not be out of place. But try it the simple way first.

For an appreciation of bubble and squeak, you need to understand the British way of life, which, until very recently, revolved around washing day. Clothes were washed on Mondays. Washing machines came late to the British Empire, so doing the laundry was a day-long endeavour which involved getting up early, boiling vast quantities of water, scrubbing, rinsing and wringing out clothes and hanging them out on the line to dry . . . just as they still do in east Vancouver. It was backbreaking, exhausting, women's work, and at the end of the day children and husbands came home expecting to eat.

Sunday was traditionally a day of rest *and* the day of the roast. A large lump of meat went into the oven surrounded by roast potatoes and vast quantities of cabbage or Brussels sprouts. The meat could be pork, lamb or beef, but the vegetables were always the same.

On Mondays — washing day — supper always consisted of leftovers from Sunday: cold, thinly sliced meat with pickled onions, cold roast potatoes, sometimes served with mustard, and heaps of . . . cabbage.

Most good recipes come out of what happens to be at hand. So it was with bubble and squeak. Some bright woman chopped up the potatoes, mixed them with the cabbage, added some pepper and salt and used an egg to stick it all together. Fried in a pan over medium heat (not too hot because she didn't want it to burn while she was getting the laundry off the line), it developed a crust on the bottom. Flipped over, it developed a crust on the other side. It sounds like nothing, but it tastes quite wonderful — the closest thing there is to British soul food.

I make it with leftover mashed potatoes, a finely chopped onion, cold, lightly cooked cabbage and an egg. The only spices are pepper and salt. A little chopped ham or crumbled bacon makes it a bigger dish, a few chopped chestnuts make it exotic and a few shrimp make it almost vegetarian. And there is no cabbage dish that can't be improved by the addition of a few caraway seeds. But even simple and unadorned, it is an extraordinarily satisfying dish.

If you're worried about what your gourmet club will say, call it *colcannon* as the Irish do, or *el trinxat cerda* as the Basques do, or even *lo bak gow*, a Cantonese variation that calls for long white radishes instead of potatoes.

And if you want further, more classical support for these simple dishes, mention Johann Sebastian Bach's preoccupation with and love for cabbage. According to musical historians, his "Goldberg Variations" were originally based on an old German folksong: "Cabbage makes you happy, and cabbage makes you fart . . . ."

Both true.

BUBBLE AND SQUEAK

leftover mashed potato
1 onion, finely chopped
cold, lightly cooked cabbage
(leftovers is fine)
1 egg
pepper and salt

Mix all the ingredients together and fry in a pan over medium heat until it develops a crust on the bottom. Flip it over and fry the other side. Extra additions could be a little chopped ham or crumbled bacon, a few chopped chestnuts, a few caraway seeds or even a few shrimp.

Pork and Prejudice

By overcoming bad press,
the Three Little Pigs have regained
their place at the dinner table.

Pork chops, kids, some dogs and the occasional cat all respond to love, attention and nourishment — particularly pork chops and kids. But while kids take time to develop (time, love, money, tears and the keys to the car), pork chops, given minimal encouragement, can come to full maturity in 20 minutes. Plain and simple, they go into a hot pan with a tablespoon of oil and almost immediately turn brown. Three minutes on each side and they are as suntanned and relaxed as your best friends back from a week in Hawaii.

But six minutes is not enough. With another 15 on medium heat they will be ready, fit partners for the North American traditionals of peas and mashed potatoes — pork chops plain and pure, pork chops Prairie style, boarding house style, the sort of pork chops that made loggers strong in the arm and tugboat men, bucking a flood tide in the Yuclataw Rapids, strong in the stomach.

Badly done, as most of them were in camps and on tugboats, these simplest of pork chops were a dry and leathery guarantee of indigestion. Apple sauce came as an antidote. It was sweet and moist and readily available, and while it was "dainty" (a quality very important at the tables of 30 years ago), it wasn't so fancy that a red-blooded man would feel embarassed when he came in from a hard day of being a red-blooded man and sat down to eat with the family.

Tidy cooks discovered that a lid on the pan not only stopped the spatters, but also made the chops more tender. Onions cooked alongside didn't burn but turned sugary and brown, and pretty soon there were tomatoes sneaking in, or sliced potatoes with a few caraway seeds, even celery cut up into two-inch lengths, a handful of oregano and some lemon juice to make (or almost make) a Greek fricassee.

Almost overnight pork became sophisticated and moved from the farm to the city. Large pork roasts shoved prime ribs of beef off dining tables and into the obscurity of steak houses. "Success, success!" cried the Three Little Pigs . . . and then came the Wolf, big and awfully bad, whose name, whispered in doctors' offices, was *Cholesterol*.

That was almost the end of pork, of chops and ham and loins and shoulders. The image of pigs was fat — nobody ever did draw a skinny one — and there was no escaping the bad press. Their name, quite understandably, was mud.

But they fought back, joined Weight Watchers, changed their diet, went to bed early and swore off candy. (Very few of them had ever smoked.) They went into politics, got to be friends with the Minister of Agriculture, had a few scientisis to dinner and instead of jiggling they jogged. Their best friends (and you have to be very special to be best friends with a pig) were amazed. "We wouldn't have known you," they said.

So the pigs sent out a Christmas card, just like everybody else. Not exactly a card with holly on it, but one of those letters about the new car and Sean doing so well in the little league and Shelagh who will soon be walking. Most of those letters have photographs stapled to the top left-hand corners, but the pigs, perhaps because they were still being fitted for their new slim-line bikinis, just typed their new dimensions very neatly and had the whole thing stamped with Agriculture Canada's official seal of approval. Less fat than lean lamb or lean beef, less fat even than trout, and less cholesterol than cheese, cod or chicken, "The New Lean Meat" was the collective title the pigs gave themselves. "In the flesh, tonight and every night: *Twiggy the Piggy!*"

The preview looked fine. It tasted like the good old days and it looked like the good old days. It also cost a little less than it used to when it was top of the bill. So if this is the new pork — The New Lean Meat or The Other White Meat — it's time we dropped our prejudices and started to cook it again.

So, some simple recipes. About three-quarters of the restaurants which offer veal in schnitzels, saltimbocca or goulash don't use veal at all, because it's so expensive. They use pork, and have done so for years — slightly flattened with a meat pounder or a bottle and then soaked in milk for a couple of hours before cooking. Nobody knows, and 90 percent of the people can't tell the difference, so file this under Money-Saving Secrets.

Pork chops and apple juice is a lovely winter dish of absolute simplicity, a dish originally cooked in Normandy, where, just like in British Columbia, they grow lots of apples as well as lots of pigs. First brown the chops in a minimum of oil (maybe a tablespoon), with the heat and the fan on high. Shove them to one side, turn the heat down to medium and quickly fry a couple of apples, sliced as thick as your finger, until they're just coloured. Push them to one side (stand the chops and slices around the side of the pan or put them on a plate) and fry a large, sliced onion until it's nicely coloured.

Sprinkle the apple slices with cinnamon and layer the onions, chops and apple slices, finishing with a few onions. Sprinkle a little pepper and salt and a healthy teaspoon of dried basil or thyme in the middle.

PORK CHOPS AND APPLES

See Page 78 for recipe.

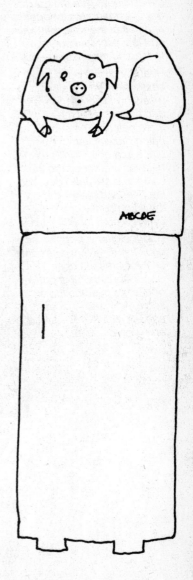

PORK AND CLAMS PORTUGUESE-STYLE

2 lb shoulder pork, cubed
2 lb clams
3 tbsp olive oil
1 bottle dry, white wine
3 cloves garlic, chopped
1 onion, chopped
1 tsp marjoram
1 tsp paprika
1 tsp pepper
salt
parsley or cilantro, chopped

Marinate the pork in a non-metallic bowl with the garlic, paprika, marjoram, pepper and half of the wine. Stir well and leave for 24 hours, turning occasionally.

Heat the oil in a deep casserole. Drain the pork, reserving the marinade, and add the cubes to the oil in three batches. As each batch browns, remove and place in a bowl. When all the batches are done, add the onion and stir until limp. Add the pork and marinade, put the lid on tightly and cook over low heat for 30 minutes.

Add the clams, re-cover and cook for 10 - 15 minutes until all the clams are open. Sprinkle a handful of parsley or cilantro over the top and serve. Add salt if necessary and serve with fresh bread and a green salad.

Now pour a cup of apple juice over everything, cover tightly and cook on top of the stove at low heat or bake in a 300°F oven for 30 minutes.

Tarragon goes well with pork, as do thyme, rosemary and, most particularly, garlic. Pork is the most accommodating of all meats; it will support almost any invention you care to come up with. Whatever's in the cupboard goes with pork. Wine, apple juice, orange or cranberry juice, grapes, orange segments, cherry tomatoes, brandy, rye, scotch, vodka or even beer — any or all of them can go into the pan to cook alongside and flavour the pork. Cheap cuts of pork cook as well as the more expensive. Pork is pork.

Pork and clams is one of my favourite winter dishes, a Portuguese classic which will amaze and delight any company you feed it to and will offer a pleasant change from the excesses of the Christmas season. You'll need one kilogram (two pounds) of shoulder pork, one kilogram of clams, a bottle of dry white wine, three cloves of garlic, an onion, one teaspoon each of marjoram, paprika and pepper plus a little salt.

Cut the meat into cubes as big as the end of your thumb and put them in a non-metallic bowl with the chopped garlic, paprika, marjoram and pepper. Add half of the wine, stir well and leave to marinate for 24 hours, turning occasionally.

The next day, when your company is actually in the house and getting serious about the peanuts, stuffed celery and vegetable dip, heat three tablespoons of olive oil in a deep casserole until it is almost smoking. Drain the pork, reserving the marinade, and add the cubes to the oil in three batches. As each batch browns, remove it from the casserole and place it in a bowl. When all the cubes are done add a chopped onion and stir until it's limp. Add the pork and the marinade (including all the bits of garlic), put the lid on tightly and cook over low heat for 30 minutes, until the pork is tender. Add the clams, recover and cook for 10 or 15 minutes until all of the clams are open and the juices have mixed with the pork. Chop a handful of cilantro, or Chinese parsley, and sprinkle it over the top. Add salt if you need to and serve with good bread and a green salad. Anything left over will reheat nicely for lunch the next day.

A Good, Honest Deal

Inexpensive cuts of meat can be a flavourful change of pace.

My mother was a young bride — an *innocent* young bride. She knew nothing of the world, and in the manner of young women of her time, she married a man who she assumed knew everything. He paid the bills, told her how to vote and, most important, he bought the meat. Every Saturday he went to the butcher and every Sunday we sat down to a leg of lamb. "A nice leg of lamb," he would say to the butcher while my mother stood there and smiled approval.

After two years of lamb she decided it was time for a change. *She* would buy the meat. She got to the butcher's the minute his shop opened, while my father was still asleep.

"Good morning, ma'am," said the butcher. "Nice leg of lamb, as usual?"

"No thank you, butcher. I'd like something different. I'd like a nice leg of . . . *beef.*"

Ten seconds later, before an audience of grinning customers, the butcher staggered out of the cooler with a 150-pound hindquarter of beef on his shoulder.

"Take it with you, ma'am? Or shall I get the boy to deliver it?"

My mother went home in tears, and until I left home we continued to eat a nice leg of lamb every Sunday. She never bought meat again, except for sausages, which were safe.

I watch people buying safe meat almost every time I go to the market. The nice, flavourful, cheap bits are passed over in favour of chops, steaks and even hamburger, and all too often people who have stood for five minutes pondering over oxtails will end up buying bologna. Short ribs, lamb ribs, veal breasts and lamb shanks are all suspect. They're not really *meat,* they're not good enough for company and besides that, "I don't have an easy recipe for them." So people pay an extra dollar per pound for pork shoulder cut up into stew when they could take it home in the piece, make 15 or 20 cuts with a knife and not only have pieces exactly the right size for the evening stew, but have enough left over to make country sausage.

Country sausage is easy. Just throw a few cubes of pork into the food processor along with a spoonful of bread crumbs, a little onion,

COUNTRY SAUSAGE

1 lb (0.5 kg) pork, cubed.
1 spoonful breadcrumbs
half an onion
salt and pepper
thyme

Put all the ingredients into a blender or food processor and whiz for a few seconds. Pat into little flat cakes and fry for breakfast.

PORK AND CELERY STEW

3 lb pork shoulder, cubed
1 head of celery, cut into finger-length pieces
1 large onion (or 2 medium), coarsely chopped
1 clove garlic, chopped
2 - 3 tbsp oil
salt and pepper
1 bay leaf
1 tsp oregano (optional)
juice of half a lemon (optional)

Heat a pan, add the oil and when hot, fry the meat in batches until lightly browned. Remove each batch as it cooks. Fry the onion and cook until starting to brown, add the garlic and stir. Add a little salt and a generous amount of pepper. Put back the meat and add the bay leaf and hot water enough to cover and simmer on top of the stove for 30 minutes.

Add the celery and mix well. Replace the lid and cook for another 20 minutes. Add 1 tsp oregano and the juice of half a lemon and cook for a further 5 minutes or add an avgolemono sauce as in the recipe below using stock from the stew pot.

some salt and pepper and a bit of whatever herb happens to be on hand — thyme is nice with ground pork. Whizz it a few seconds and then pat it into little fat cakes, which you fry for breakfast. A few slices of apple fried in the pan and sprinkled with cinnamon will bring your family to look at you with respect and admiration. Much cheaper than bacon, and much nicer.

Since we've got the pork, and we're bathed in the glow of self-righteous virtue that comes from a perfectly honest good deal, that special virtue that gives food that old-fashioned grandma flavour, let's look at a couple of different things to do with it. So, you've got about three pounds of pork shoulder or pork butt, whatever's cheap, enough to feed six and have a bit left over for tomorrow.

Celery is cheap in winter. Cut a good-sized head into finger-length pieces. Cut one large or two medium onions into a dozen pieces and flatten a clove of garlic. Cut the meat into cubes as big as walnuts, and heat two or three tablespoons of oil in whatever pot you use for making stew. Remember that if you put cold oil into a cold pan and then heat it, food will stick. But if you are clever and knowledgeable (as well as especially virtuous) you will heat the pan first and then put the oil in, which nine times out of 10 will prevent sticking. I don't know why, but that's the way it is.

When the oil is hot, fry the meat cubes a few at a time, giving each side a chance to become seared, or lightly browned. This seals the outsides so the juices stay in, giving the meat flavour and tenderness. Take the cubes out as they cook and put a few more in. If any *do* stick, don't worry — they'll come off while the stew is cooking and give it even more flavour.

After you've cooked the meat, put in the onion and cook it until there are slight signs of browning. Now add the garlic and stir for a minute. Add salt with discretion and pepper with generosity, then put the meat back, along with a bay leaf. Almost cover with hot water, cover and simmer on top of the stove for 30 minutes. Now add the celery and mix it well with the pork, which shouldn't be completely cooked because a special flavour develops when it cooks with celery. Put the lid back on and cook another 20 minutes.

Now you have a lot of choices. Add a good-sized teaspoon of oregano and the juice of half a lemon and cook another five minutes. That's one way to do it. Or you can be extremely Greek and make an *avgolemono* sauce, which is a lot easier than it sounds.

Separate two eggs and beat the yolks for two minutes with a whisk, a fork or the machine. Now add the juice of a lemon, drop by drop, still beating continuously. Spoon a tablespoon of hot stock out of the stew pot and with a wooden spoon slowly stir it into the lemon and egg mixture. And again. And again. And again, until the sauce is just warm. Take the stew off the stove, get everybody to the table, stir in the *avgolemono,* sprinkle well with chopped parsley and serve the stew with rice or steamed potatoes.

Like all stews, it's better the next day, but if you're doing it for company don't make the *avgolemono* until a few minutes before you serve it. A little green dill is nice, as well as (or instead of) the oregano, and if you want a change, the recipe works equally well with lamb or veal.

If you want a fancy dinner, you'll need some kind of Greek starter — not a soup, because the stew is already liquid. Greek mushrooms are ridiculously easy. Cut the stems off a pound of small, fresh mushrooms. Boil two cups of water with a little salt, add the mushroom caps and simmer no more than two minutes. Drain off the water and put the caps in a jar or bowl.

Make a marinade by boiling a quarter-cup of olive oil with a half-cup of vinegar, a teaspoon of peppercorns and a teaspoons dried oregano or thyme. Pour the marinade over the mushrooms and let them cool to lukewarm. That's it. They'll keep covered in the fridge for three or four days. A lemon, thinly sliced and arranged over the top, makes for considerable elegance.

AVGOLEMONO SAUCE

2 eggs
juice of a lemon
1 cup hot stock

Separate the eggs and beat the yolks for 2 minutes with a whisk, fork or machine. Add the lemon juice, drop by drop, beating continuously. Stir a tablespoon of hot stock slowly into the lemon and egg mixture using a wooden spoon. Keep adding a tablespoon at a time and stirring until the sauce is just warm. Add to the stew or soup.

GREEK MUSHROOMS

1 lb small, fresh mushrooms, stems removed
2 cups water
salt
1/4 cup olive oil
1/2 cup vinegar
1 tsp peppercorns
1 tsp dried oregano or thyme
1 lemon

Boil the water with a little salt. Add the mushroom caps and simmer for 2 minutes. Drain and put the caps into a jar or bowl.

Make a marinade by boiling the olive oil, vinegar, peppercorns, oregano or thyme. Pour this over the mushrooms and let them cool to lukewarm. Keep covered in the fridge for up to four days. Decorate with a thinly sliced lemon.

Cozy Up To Chowder

All you really need is a big pot and some bacon bits. After that, you improvise.

BASIC CHOWDER

4 oz bacon bits
1 carrot, thinly sliced
2 sticks celery, thinly sliced
1 onion, coarsely chopped
1 bay leaf
2 - 3 cloves garlic
1 tsp pepper

Fry the bacon in a large pot and remove. Add the carrot and celery and cook over medium heat for 2 minutes. Add the onion, bay leaf and whole cloves of garlic. Stir and add the pepper.

CLAM CHOWDER

2 medium potatoes, diced
1/2 bunch parsley, finely chopped
1 tsp dried (or few sprigs of fresh) dill
1 large can of clams, including the juice
salt
lemon juice
1/2 cup cream
grated nutmeg

Add to the Basic Chowder, the potatoes, parsley, dill, clam juice and enough water to cover everything. Simmer for 20 minutes. Add the clams, some salt, lemon juice, cream and a sprinkling of grated nutmeg. A glass of sherry or rye can be added for a little more sophistication.

In most supermarkets, almost every deli and all proper butcher shops, there is always — and it is sometimes as hard to find as the object of this sentence — a tray, the least attractive of all trays. It's slightly scruffy and disorganized, a great contrast to the orderly rows of pork chops, the carefully stacked schnitzels, the steaks, the sausages and the tenderloins all so regimented and tidy.

In this tray is meat, as jumbled and confused as a laundry room on Monday. Not just ordinary meat, but meat ridiculously cheap, meat full of solid, rich flavour, more potent and pervasive than any soup cubes you can buy. Meat which most people are ashamed to be seen with because they have been taught that real food has to have a proper name and a proper shape so that is can be identified in a recipe by number, like four lamb chops and three cloves of garlic, one medium onion or one-sixteenth of a teaspoon of paprika.

So it sits there, waiting for the little old ladies with the big purses and the European accents, and we go home with our carefully made shopping lists, every item and every recipe checked against a master plan, because *company's coming,* and we are stuck with the tyranny of the formal recipe which defines The Only Way To Do It in a form as exact, and frequently as exciting, as a prescription from the doctor.

We stick to the recipes, and we don't improvise because we're scared. That's why we don't buy the stuff in the tray — the bacon bits, the salami cutoffs and the ham ends. The recipe calls for three slices of bacon or four ounces (100 grams) of ham, so we usually go out and buy exactly that. The recipe then says, "Chop it fine, and fry it." By the time we've got that done, we have a pan full of ham or bacon bits and a lot of melted fat, which is exactly what we would have had if we'd chopped up four ounces of the scraps and cutoffs, which cost at most a quarter of what we've paid for the "real" stuff.

Paying less is not only the key to good peasant cooking — it's also a great escape into the joys of improvisation, because you can afford to make a mistake. So the next time you see a tray of bacon bits or salami ends, buy some and bring them home in triumph. You'll have the beginnings of a whole series of chowders — corn chowder, chicken chowder, clam chowder. All of them start with the same instruction: "Fry a little chopped bacon in the bottom of a good, big pot."

All real cooks have a big pot — aluminum, enamel, stainless steel or the big cast-iron one from the Prairie grandma. It's the symbol of emancipation and real domesticity: no more pigging it straight from the frypan it was cooked in, no more TV dinners or microwaved marvels. The big pot means spaghetti, or two dozen ears of corn. It means supper for the whole soccer team or a Saturday afternoon spent making chicken stock. People with big pots really intend, no matter how things turn out later, to *stay* married.

So you've got four ounces of bacon bits in the pot, fried over medium heat until they smell good. Fish out the meat scraps and put them aside. Now add a thinly sliced carrot to the pot and cook it, still at medium heat, with a couple of sticks of thinly sliced celery. After a couple of minutes add a coarsely chopped onion, a bay leaf and two or three whole cloves of garlic. Stir it all together with a wooden spoon, add about a teaspoon of pepper and in five minutes you have the basis of your chowder. At this time you may reflect on the fact that our word chowder comes from the French *chaudron,* which simply means a big cooking pot, and that you are doing what generations of French cooks have done in making something simple, cheap and wonderful for supper.

Clam chowder? Add two medium potatoes diced a little smaller than sugar cubes, about half a bunch of finely chopped parsley, about a teaspoon of dried (or a few sprigs of fresh) green dill and the juice from a large can of clams. Add enough water to cover everything and let it simmer for 20 minutes. Add the clams, a little more chopped parsley, some salt and a little lemonn juice. You can say the chowder is now complete. But if you're looking for perfection, add a half-cup of cream. Exotica? Stir in a teaspoon of curry powder and the juice of half a lemon. Sophistication? A sprinkling of grated nutmeg. A glass of sherry never hurt anything in a pot, least of all a chowder, nor, for that matter, did a couple of ounces of rye. If three or four uninvited guests arrive it's best to turn it into a Manhattan chowder, which means adding a can of plum tomatoes (usually better value and more flavourful than the fresh tomatoes of winter), another potato, a little extra pepper and some thyme or oregano. Whatever you do to it from now on, it's chowder — a big, hot pot of it.

Chicken chowder? Start with the bacon bits, onion, garlic, carrot, celery, pepper, parsley and bay leaf, just like before. Cook it three or four minutes, then add a cut-up chicken, three cloves, eight cups of water and some green dill. Cover and let it simmer 30 minutes. Add 3 medium potatoes and cook another 15 minutes. Meanwhile, melt a lump of butter in a frypan, add a cup of sliced mushrooms and cook

MANHATTAN CHOWDER

1 can plum tomatoes
1 medium potato, diced
pepper
thyme or oregano

Add to the Clam Chowder the tomatoes, the extra potato, some extra pepper and some thyme or oregano.

CHICKEN CHOWDER

1 chicken, cut-up
3 cloves
8 cups water
dill
3 medium potatoes, diced
butter
1 cup mushrooms, sliced
2 tbsp flour
1 tsp curry powder
1/2 cup cream
1 glass sherry or rye
parsley, chopped

Add to the Basic Chowder the chicken, cloves, water and dill. Cover and simmer for 30 minutes. Add the potatoes and cook for a further 15 minutes. Meanwhile melt a lump of butter in a frypan, add the mushrooms and cook for 3 minutes. Add the flour, curry powder and cook for 3 minutes. Stir the mushrooms into the chowder and let cook for 2 minutes. Add the cream and sherry or rye. Sprinkle w chopped parsley.

CHICKEN AND CORN CHOWDER

1 can corn (creamed or whole kernel) or fresh corn scraped from the cob

Cook as for Chicken Chowder but substitute the corn for the 3 diced potatoes.

FISH CHOWDER

3 potatoes, thinly sliced
1 kg inexpensive fish
4 oz bacon bits
fish stock
1 onion, coarsely chopped
2 - 3 cloves garlic
1 red pepper, diced
1 green pepper, diced
2 bay leaves
1 tsp dried thyme
2 small, hot, red peppers
salt and black pepper
1 tsp chili powder
juice of a lemon or lime
1 can tomatoes
parsley, chopped
1 glass of rye

For the fish stock simmer about 1 lb of fish heads, bones and trimmings in a pot for 30 minutes with a bay leaf and some peppercorns. Strain off the liquid and throw out the bones. Or you can use apple juice, light beer, dry cider or canned clam juice.

Fry the bacon bits and remove. Add the onion and whole cloves of garlic. Add the peppers, thyme, bay leaves, hot peppers, chili powder, lemon or lime juice, tomatoes, salt and pepper. Cook for 15 minutes.

Add the potatoes and bring to a boil, add the fish, cover with fish stock and cook no longer than 10 minutes. Sprinkle with a lot of chopped parsley and add the rye.

for three minutes. Add two tablespoons of flour and one teaspoon of curry powder and cook together for another three minutes. Stir the mushrooms into the chowder, let it cook for a couple of minutes and then add some cream — and/or sherry or rye. Sprinkle with a little parsley and once again you have chowder — chicken chowder.

Chicken and corn chowder? Same as chicken chowder, but instead of potatoes add either a can of corn (creamed or whole kernel) or, even better, fresh corn scraped from the cob with a sharp knife. (Do it over a plate to collect the milk.) Mushrooms, cream, curry powder — everything's the same as the chicken chowder, but there is a particular velvety magic in the combination of chicken and corn. Sometimes I float dumplings in the chowder for the last 15 minutes.

Fish chowder? Most recipes call for a half-pound of salt pork, cubed and fried. Use a handful of bacon bits instead. You will also need some fish stock. It's simply fish heads, bones and timmings simmered for 30 minutes in the big pot with a bay leaf and some peppercorns, the liquid strained off and the bones thrown out (unless you put them in the Cuisinart and feed them to the cat).

Fry the bacon, lift out the meat and pour off all the fat except for a couple of tablespoons. Add the onions and garlic just as you did making clam chowder, but instead of a carrot use a couple of diced peppers, one red and one green. Instead of dill use thyme, add two bay leaves instead of one and throw in a couple of those small, hot red peppers. Add some black pepper, a teaspoon of chili powder, the juice of a lime or lemon, a little salt and a can of tomatoes and cook it all for 15 minutes.

Meanwhile, thinly slice three potatoes and put them in cold water to stop them from turning brown. Add them to the pot, bring to a boil and then add the fish. Cover with stock and cook no longer than 10 minutes from the time it boils. Sprinkle with a lot of chopped parsley and, since by now you may have gotten into the habit, an ounce or two of rye. Fish chowders need a little more salt than do chicken or clam chowders. If you can't be bothered making the fish stock, use apple juice. Or light beer. Or dry cider. The only absolutely necessary things are the big pots and the bacon bits.

Conducting The Early Morning Symphony

Try a new tune at the breakfast table and you'll get a standing ovation.

Bacon and eggs, orange juice and intravenous coffee: the traditional North American breakfast. When I was a businessman we met at seven in the morning, shaved down to the bone and shoes shined, and by eight o'clock it was time for the Tums, with the world nicely arranged to revolve around our little profits. The next morning, in Vancouver, Calgary or Toronto, we would rerun it — bacon, eggs, orange juice and coffee, good ol' J.B. talking to good ol' C.J. And so it went until Saturday, when the kids would get up and we'd all have breakfast together — bacon, eggs, orange juice and coffee, because the essence of tradition is repetition and familiarity, just like turkey at Christmas and pumpkin pie at Thanksgiving. I've eaten bacon and eggs in greasy spoons, in logging camps, on trains, fishboats and airplanes.

A good friend of mine, a criminal lawyer — a cool, unemotional, critical and careful-minded woman — was overcome with pity for a man whose kitchen consisted of a frypan on a Coleman stove. On the stove sat the black iron frypan and in the pan sat a fried egg, black lace around the edges, very cold and very old, in a lake of congealed bacon fat — the ultimate statement of incompetent bachelorhood. She married him, cooked him bacon and eggs every morning in a shining copper pan and served them on bright yellow plates before she went off to the office.

Six months later he left her — not for another woman, but for bacon and eggs the way he liked them: greasy, overcooked, burned on the bottom, hard, cold and slapped between two slices of white bread. Habit dies hard, and bacon and eggs are particularly addictive. Even the Emperor of Japan, who lives in a palace surrounded by a lake with a hundred gardeners to look after the cherry blossoms, has bacon and eggs (after porridge) for his breakfast every morning.

The real importance of breakfast is not *what* you eat, but how you eat it and with whom you make it. Mom, who used to be the conductor of the early morning symphony, now has as much trouble finding her briefcase or her workboots as anybody else. Automatic coffee makers, toaster waffles and Egg McMuffins have turned weekday breakfast into a family version of an Indianapolis pit stop. Weekends aren't much

FISH CAKES

cold, mashed potato
equal amount of cold,
cooked fish (or canned tuna)
1 medium onion, finely
chopped
1 egg
a handful of chopped
parsley
salt and pepper
breadcrumbs or flour

*Mix all the ingredients
together vigorously and roll
into balls as large as eggs.
Flatten each one into a
round cake as thick as your
finger. Pat breadcrumbs or
flour onto each side and fry
them crisp and brown over
medium heat. Eat with
ketchup or Worcestershire
sauce.*

PSEUDO-PSOURDOUGH PANCAKES

3 eggs
6 oz plain yoghurt
1 cup milk
1 cup flour
2 tbsp sugar
1 tsp salt
2 tsp baking powder
1 tsp baking soda
4 tbsp oil or melted butter

*Beat the eggs in a bowl and
then beat in the yoghurt, milk
and flour. When smooth beat
in the remaining ingredients.
Let the mixture stand for 10
minutes then cook, as for
pancakes, one side at a time
in a lightly greased frypan
over medium heat. Serve
with a little melted butter and
real maple syrup.*

better. Soccer, shopping, ballet classes and walking the gerbil all take precedence over breakfast, and we finish up trying to remember whether we have two kids or three and the name of the person we married.

Gourmet magazines talk about breakfast as a romantic event — candles, champagne, a bubble bath and infinite variations of eggs Benedict. Only the desperate will attempt eggs Benedict, which is best made in the kitchen of an expensive restaurant where the cook who makes the hollandaise doesn't have to toast the muffins, grill the ham or, most important, poach the eggs to exactly the right softness. Good eggs Benedict needs at least four hands.

But there are alternatives. Hotcakes out of a package taste like everything else out of a package — they have flat, uninspiring taste of "easy." Real hotcakes, may take five minutes more than the premixed ones, but their memory (and your reputation) will last a lifetime.

Pseudo-psourdough pancakes are quite simply the best in the world. They have the same subtle acidity as real sourdough, without any of the hassles of yeast. They are rich and fluffy, and above all they are simple, the sort of real cooking that children love to do — and *can* do.

Beat three eggs in a bowl, then beat in 200 millilitres (six ounces) of plain yogurt, one cup of milk and one cup of flour. When it's smooth, beat in two tablespoons of sugar, one teaspoon of salt, two teaspoons of baking powder, one teaspoon of baking soda, and four tablespoons of oil or melted butter.

Let the mixture stand for 10 minutes while you make coffee or squeeze oranges or talk to the kids, then cook the pancakes like you would any other pancakes, one side at a time in a lightly greased frypan over medium heat. The pancakes don't need to be stacked. Just serve them as they come out of the pan, one at a time, with a little melted butter and real maple syrup.

Fish cakes are another magnificent breakfast — yesterday's cold mashed potatoes and an equal quantity of cold, cooked, cheap fish (even canned tuna will do), a finely chopped onion, some pepper, chopped parsley and an egg, all squished together by hand or zipped through a couple of bursts in the food processor. Roll the mixture into balls as big as plums, flatten them as thick as your finger, pat breadcrumbs into both sides, fry them crisp and almost dark brown over medium heat and eat with ketchup or Worcestershire sauce.

But fish cakes take second place to corned beef hash, a real family dish which everybody can help make. It tastes great hot and almost as good cold for lunch. I first made it in France, in a tin plate with stolen potatoes and the canned corned beef which the army thought essential to the care and feeding of young soldiers. With canned or fresh meat, it is an extraordinarily simple, honest and filling dish which you may well promote from breakfast to family supper.

You need 200 grams (six ounces) of finely chopped fresh corned beef, or one can of crumbled corned beef. Add one finely chopped medium onion, three coarsely grated medium potatoes, one egg and a few good sprinkles of black pepper. Squish everything together with your hands, squeezing it through your fingers. (Children love to do this.) Oil a frypan, pat the hash in with a fork and sprinkle one and a half teaspoons of dry mustard over it. Cook over medium heat for about 10 minutes, then turn it over by sliding it out onto a plate and flipping it. Sprinkle more mustard on top and cook another 10 minutes. There will be a thick brown crust on both sides and a lovely rich smell in the kitchen. It's a great breakfast for a bunch of hungry kids, and very sophisticated if you put a poached egg on each serving.

Eggs in a nest is a very, very simple and very, very satisfying dish. Cut a circle out of a slice of bread with a wine glass and fry the bread (and the circle) on one side. Turn the bread over and break an egg into the hole. Sprinkle with a little pepper and salt and cook until the white is set and the yolk is soft. The cut-out circle can be propped up against the side with a toothpick through it, like a wagon wheel, or it can be decorated with a sprig of parsley or a slice of fried tomato, but the real trick to it is making sure the bread can be dipped in the yolk. There is a small child in all of us . . . .

Good porridge is best on a wet morning. You need oats — not the quick oats, but the slow-cooking ones, cooked according to the package directions. The difference is about 15 minutes, and during those 15 minutes, everybody makes the big decision as to what else will go in during the last three minutes of cooking. Chopped dried apricots are wonderfully piquant, chopped nuts (any kind — walnuts, hazelnuts or almonds, lightly roasted to crisp them up), sesame seeds, raisins, diced apples, slices of ripe banana, chunks of kiwi fruit, strawberries, chopped dried figs — use any or all of them. Sprinkle the porridge with brown sugar and eat it with milk, not cream. Cream is too rich and masks the textures and flavours of everything else.

So don't avoid breakfast simply because you can't face bacon and eggs, orange juice or coffee. The easiest way to make breakfast a habit is to make it a surprise.

CORNED BEEF HASH

6 oz fresh corned beef, finely chopped (or 1 can crumbled corn beef)
1 medium onion, finely chopped
3 medium potatoes, coarsely grated
1 egg
a few sprinkles black pepper
dry mustard

Mix all the ingredients together with your hands, giving it a good squeeze. Oil a frypan, pat the hash in with a fork and sprinkle 1-1/2 tsp dry mustard over the top. Cook over medium heat for about 10 minutes. Turn it over (slide it out onto a plate and flip it), sprinkle more mustard on top and cook for another 10 minutes. Serve with a poached egg on each serving.

EGG IN A NEST

1 egg
1 slice bread
salt and pepper

Cut a circle out of the slice of bread with a wine glass and fry the bread (and the circle) on one side. Turn the bread over and break an egg into the hole. Sprinkle with a little salt and pepper and cook until the white is set and the yolk is soft. Serve with the cut-out circle propped up against the side with a toothpick through it or decorated with a sprig of parsley or a slice of fried tomato.

Eggstra Simple, Eggstra Special

Uncomplicated ways to give eggs a starring role.

HUEVOS RANCHEROS

1 large onion, finely chopped
2 - 3 cloves garlic, finely
chopped
3 - 4 ripe tomatoes, roughly
chopped (1 can tomatoes)
2 tbsp oil
2 tsp flour
4 tsp chili powder
1 tsp mint
1 tsp salt
1 tsp sage
a little tomato paste
2 cups water
2 eggs (per person)

Fry the onion over medium heat in the oil, stirring occasionally. When the onions are soft, stir in the garlic, cook for 1 minute and add the tomatoes.

Mix (or shake up in a bottle) the flour, chili powder, mint, sage, salt, tomato paste and 2 - 3 tbsp water until it's smooth. Pour into the pan with 2 cups of water, stir and let simmer for 20 minutes stirring occasionally.

Crack the eggs, two at a time, into a saucer and slide them into the simmering sauce. Poach until the whites are set and the yolks are soft. Remove them with a spatula and serve with a little of the sauce.

For a large amount, pour the sauce into a baking tin, slide the eggs into the sauce and bake in a 350°F oven until they're ready.

On the west coast of Mexico, at the mouth of a little river, there is a fishing village called Zihuatenejo where for six dollars a night, on the poor people's side of the bridge, you can still find a hotel room. Not the greatest hotel room in the world — no hot water, no carpets, no phone, no television and certainly no room-service. But there is a wake-up service. Every morning at dawn, five minutes before the fishermen crank up their outboards, the rooster cranks up his vocal chords and struts around every window (there are no curtains, either), hustling everybody into some sort of activity, even if it's working hard to get back to sleep.

Everybody in Mexican villages has chickens. Poor people always have chickens. Country people usually have chickens, and they all sympathize with them. They understand chickens, even if they don't call them by their first names, and they know what they are for: to eat as little as possible, lay as many eggs as possible and, when they are very, very old, go into the stew pot.

But city people really only know chickens when they're fried, roasted, in a clubhouse sandwich or sitting on a supermarket shelf. And eggs, to city people, are usually a last resort for those times when there's nothing else in the house. Eggs have their moments of glory when fashion dictates angel food cake ("Take one dozen eggs . . .") or quiche ("For sophisticated entertainment, the fashionable housewife . . ."), but the egg as a soloist never quite made it into the top 10, never achieved recognition without expensive accompaniments. Eggs Benedict, for example, needs ham and muffins and hollandaise sauce, and eggs Sardou can't exist without artichokes and champagne.

But the Mexicans give their eggs the full dignity of a starring role. *Huevos rancheros* is an easy dish and, like most peasant cooking, best when it's simplest. If you make too much sauce, use it tomorrow on pasta, freeze it for another day or eat it with sausages. You can even put it on toast. And if somebody arrives unexpectedly, open the freezer and dump the sauce in a pan with a little water, and in five minutes . you've got supper almost made, while they look at you with that awestruck, open-mouthed admiration usually reserved for Albert Einstein.

As you almost always do with peasant food, you need onions and garlic. Finely chop one big onion and two or three fat cloves of garlic. Cut three or four ripe, juicy tomatoes into quarters, then halve the quarters. If you can't find good, ripe tomatoes, use canned. Fry the onions over medium heat in two tablespoons of oil (Mexicans use lard because they also have pigs, but you have a bottle because you have a supermarket), stirring occasionally. When the onions are soft and a little transparent, stir in the garlic, cook for one minute and add the tomatoes.

Now comes the complicated part, which a Mexican cook might do in a cup or clay bowl or shake up in a beer bottle. Combine two teaspoons of flour, four teaspoons of chili powder, one teaspoon each of mint, sage and salt and a little tomato paste, if you have it. Mix it all with two or three tablespoons of water until it's smooth, then pour it into the pan with two cups of water. Stir it a lot and then let it simmer for 20 minutes, stirring occasionally. If it gets too thick, add a little water. You want a sauce that is not as thick as spaghetti sauce and not as thin as soup.

Two eggs apiece is a good number for huevos rancheros. Crack them two at a time into a saucer, then slide them into the simmering sauce. Poach until the whites set and the yolks are still runny. Then remove them with a spatula and serve them with a little sauce. If you want to be a hero and do huevos rancheros for a dozen, heat the oven to 350°F, pour the sauce into a baking tin or shallow casserole, slide the eggs into the sauce and bake until they're ready. You can't do that with eggs Benedict.

The Italians have an even simpler dish called *piselli con uova*, which simply means peas and eggs. It's a lovely, quick and comforting supper dish which takes about 20 minutes. Once again, start with a chopped onion and a clove of garlic, cooked in a little olive oil for two or three minutes. Add a small can of tomatoes, complete with the juice, and cook for 10 minutes. Now add a packet of frozen peas and cook for two minutes, then salt and more pepper than you think wise and finally the eggs, which cook in the sauce for three or four minutes. Very pleasant, very simple, and if you have hungry kids, you can serve it over spaghetti.

Half a pound of sliced mushrooms, fried for three minutes in butter (they'll still look white and firm) and sprinkled with salt, pepper and a little nutmeg, is another good way to start eggs for supper. Add half a cup of cream, stir it all well together and once again slide the eggs in for three or four minutes, either in the oven or on top of the stove.

Then there's boiled eggs, the lunchbox special which usually has very little taste and the consistency of worn-out golf balls. Everybody

PISELLI CON UOVA OR PEAS WITH EGGS

1 onion, finely chopped
1 clove garlic, finely chopped
olive oil
1 small can tomatoes
1 packet frozen peas
salt and pepper
2 eggs (per person)

Fry the onion and garlic in olive oil for 2 - 3 minutes. Add the tomatoes, including the juice, and cook for 10 minutes. Add the packet of frozen peas and cook for 2 minutes, then generously sprinkle with salt and pepper. Slide the eggs into the sauce and cook for 3 - 4 minutes.

MUSHROOMS AND EGGS

1/2 lb mushrooms, sliced
1/2 cup cream
butter
salt and pepper
grated nutmeg
2 eggs (per person)

Fry the mushrooms in butter for 3 minutes. Sprinkle with salt, pepper and nutmeg. Add the cream, stir it all together, slide in the eggs and cook for 3 - 4 minutes either in the oven or on top of the stove.

ZABAGLIONE

4 eggs
2 tbsp white sugar (brown won't work)
2 - 3 oz sherry, white wine or port

Find a bowl and a saucepan over which the bowl can comfortably rest. Put water in the saucepan to boil. Separate the eggs and beat the yolks in the bowl until they're fluffy. Beat in the sugar and the sherry, white wine or port.

Turn off the heat under the boiling water, put the bowl over the water and beat the mixture vigorously with a whisk or electric beater until it thickens (about 6 - 8 minutes). Serve in your nicest glasses.

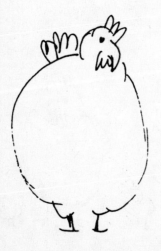

should know exactly how to boil the perfect egg, but few do, since it is a skill ignored by high school cooking teachers. So herewith, a few useful facts: brown eggs are no better than white, but because they *look* warmer and richer they seem to taste nicer. Remember (but don't tell anybody) that adding the brown skin of an onion to the water will make boiled white eggs into the most convincing brown ones. There is no nutritional benefit in this deception, but it is a certain crowd pleaser, and compliments at breakfast ("How nice, *brown* eggs!") can set you up for the rest of the day.

The actual boiling is important. Cold eggs dumped without ceremony into a pot of boiling water will usually crack and leak, losing their essential simple charm. If left to hard-boil, they will also develop a dark greeny black line between the yolk and the white. The boiled egg purist will take a small saucepan, put the eggs in it, cover them with cold water and then, over high heat, bring the water to a full, rolling boil. Immediately turn off the heat or take the pan off the electric stove. Three minutes later you will have the perfect soft-boiled egg, four minutes later the perfect medium and ten minutes later the perfect hard-boiled with just a trace of softness in the middle (what fancy French cooks call *mollet*).

Getting the shell off a hard-boiled egg can be difficult unless you plunge it into cold water immediately after it is cooked. Peel it under running water while its inside is still hot.

Finally, to help you achieve unimaginable fame as an egg cook, there is *zabaglione,* the wonderful, fluffy, sensuous dessert of which head waiters in expensive restaurants make such a production. It's cheaper than cake, quicker, easier and more digestible.

There is no need for copper pots or any fancy equipment. All you need is a bowl big enough to beat half a dozen eggs in, a whisk or an egg beater and a saucepan over which the bowl can comfortably rest. Put water in the saucepan to boil. Meanwhile, separate four eggs and beat the yolks in the bowl until they're fluffy. Now beat in two tablespoons of white sugar (brown won't work) and two or three ounces of sherry, white wine or port — whatever you have in the cupboard.

Now turn off the heat under the boiling water. Put the bowl over the water and beat the mixture vigorously with a whisk or electric beater until it thickens, which should take six to eight minutes. You just learn to smile while you beat, make intelligent conversation with your friends, breathe deeply and not appear the least bit stressed. Finally, you serve it in your nicest glasses (you don't need a great deal of it), smiling modestly.

You will never again buy commercial custard, and each time you pass eggs in the supermarket you will smile once more — a sort of Mexican smile.

Rooting For Flavour

Cooking with ginger is a snap.

There are two ways to cook, one of which is not really cooking at all, but the frantic, slavish, *worried* following of every minute detail of a recipe — how big is a pinch, and how medium is a carrot? The other way to cook is to relax, to let dinner happen, just as a sunrise happens, just a little beyond your control, always different, always marvelous, the best dinner that ever was.

That's pride, not arrogance, and it's an essential ingredient of real cooking, a much better flavour enhancer than MSG. When you sit down at the table with a great smile on your face and say, right out loud, "Damn, that's good," you *know* you're a cook. And so does everybody else at the table. You will go down in history. They'll talk about you every time they eat something extra special: "Remember when Mum/Dad/Chuck/Angie used to make that really great thing on cold days?" You won't be a chef, but you'll be a cook, and that's an important thing to be.

The sad truth is that many food writers, who don't really understand or even really *like* food, desperately try to keep up with fashion by repeating complicated procedures they have read about somewhere else, never getting down to the basics. So you go and buy an ingredient, use it once for a special recipe and find it two years later, sitting mouldy at the back of the freezer, its label unreadable. (You get to be a cook, a *real* cook, by using an ingredient a lot, in all sorts of dishes, until you understand it and it becomes familiar as pepper and salt, something you use almost without thinking.) Take ginger, which is now popping up in all kinds of recipes, complete with all kinds of fancy instructions like carefully peeling and measuring it in teaspoonsful. One writer even recommended blanching it for a couple of minutes in boiling water to remove some of the taste.

Ginger used to be sold only in Chinatown. Now it's even at 7-Eleven. It's a tan-coloured root, slight knobbly, very smooth and shiny when it's fresh and a little wrinkled when it's older. The best time to buy it is when it's fresh, when it's full of juice and flavour. It slices easily on a board with a big, sharp knife, and it grates easily on the coarse side of a grater. (The fine side clogs up.)

CHICKEN AND GINGER

1 cut up chicken
10 to 20 slices of fresh ginger
1 Tbsp cornstarch
2 tbsp oil
1 clove garlic, chopped
3 tbsp water (or wine, apple juice, cider or beer)
salt and pepper
lemon juice
parsley, chopped

Heat a frypan, add the oil and then fry the ginger slices. Dust the chicken pieces with cornstarch, push the ginger aside and fry the chicken for 2 - 3 minutes each side. Add the garlic and water, dust with pepper, put the lid on and cook over low heat for 20 minutes. Salt to taste, add a few drops of lemon juice and some chopped parsley and serve.

GINGER TEA

4 cups water
a finger-length piece of ginger, grated or chopped fine
4 tbsp sugar or honey
juice of half a lemon
4 cloves

Bring all the ingredients to a boil and simmer it, covered, for 15 minutes. Strain and drink it hot, or leave to cool and strain into a jug to keep in the fridge. Dilute with soda water and use for ginger ale.

RHUBARB AND GINGER

1 lb rhubarb, cut into thumb-size lengths
4 slices ginger, cut into matchstick strips
1/4 cup sugar
a little lemon juice

Put the ginger into a saucepan with the sugar and lemon juice and slowly melt the sugar over low heat until transparent. Add the rhubarb, cover and cook slowly for 10 minutes. Serve perhaps with a little cream or plain yoghurt.

PORK CHOPS AND GINGER

2 pork chops
1 onion, sliced
6 slices ginger, cut into matchstick strips
garlic
2 tbsp oil
apple juice
a few mushrooms, whole if small or halved if bigger
salt and pepper

Heat the pan, add the oil and quickly fry the chops over high heat until light brown on each side. Add the ginger and onion. Stir for 2 minutes and add the garlic, pepper and a little apple juice. Bring to a boil, cover and simmer over low heat for 15 minutes. Add the mushrooms, stir and cook for a further 5 minutes. Serve over rice.

So you take home a chunk of ginger about as big as a croissant, and you cut four slices off it as thick as a magazine. Now, to understand ginger, take one of these slices and rub it gently on your temples, the part of your forehead just above your eyebrows on the sides of your head. Cooling, calming, gently fragrant — this is the essence of ginger, which also works miracles with chicken and fish, fruit and vegetables, beef and pork and almost everything except eggs. Ginger has always been important in Oriental cooking, and today even French cooks, the most conservative of us all, use it regularly, not just for its flavour, but for its digestive qualities.

Let's start with chicken and ginger. When the frypan is hot, put in two tablespoons of oil. (If you put oil into a cold pan and then heat it, things will stick. I don't know why, but they will.) Cook the slices of ginger until they smell nice. Dust some chicken pieces with cornstarch, push the ginger slices aside and fry the chicken for two or three minutes a side. Add a clove of chopped garlic and three tablespoons of water (or wine or apple juice or cider or beer), dust with pepper, put the lid on and cook over low heat for 20 minutes. Salt to taste (salting chicken *before* cooking makes it tough) and serve. A few drops of lemon juice are nice and a little chopped parsley is pretty, but the real flavours is in the ginger, with its slightly spicy, slightly sugary freshness.

Next, try rhubarb and ginger. Everybody's garden and most of the markets have rhubarb. Most recipes render it bland and overly sweet, but when cooked with ginger, rhubarb's own fresh flavour comes through. The secret to maintaining its texture is not overcooking it.

Cut a pound of rhubarb into pieces as long as your thumb, and cut four slices of ginger into matchstick strips. Put the ginger into a saucepan with a quarter-cup of sugar and a little lemon juice and slowly melt the sugar over low heat until it's transparent. Add the rhubarb, cover and cook slowly for 10 minutes at most. In that time it will have cooked and developed a special flavour with the ginger, while retaining its shape. It's very nice with a little cream, or put into one of those little ice cream machines, or mixed with plain yogurt, or even cold next morning with breakfast cereal.

Ginger and pork requires two pork chops, an onion, pepper, salt, ginger, a little apple juice and some mushrooms. Heat the pan, add two tablespoons of oil and quickly fry the chops over high heat until they're light brown on each side. Cut six slices of ginger into matchsticks and add them and the sliced onion. Stir for two minutes, add the garlic and pepper, stir a bit to marry everything and add the apple juice — not too much, because there will be juices coming out of the pork and the mushrooms. Bring to a boil, turn the heat to low, cover and simmer for 15 minutes. Add the mushrooms (whole if they're small, halved or quartered if they're bigger), stir everything together and cook covered for another five minutes. Serve over rice.

Fish and ginger is another winner. Salmon, cod, halibut, even trout — the recipe is always the same. Fry matchsticks of ginger in a little oil, then flour the fish and fry it with the ginger for no more than eight minutes per inch of thickness, turning just once.

That's it. Now you can cook with ginger. Chicken, pork, fish and rhubarb. Now cook it with apples, or in a vegetable stir-fry, or with blueberries or hard pears if you have a tree. Add it to tomato soup or any vegetable soup, veal dishes, beef stews and chowders. Rub it on the insides of your wrists instead of your temples. If you find an exceptionally fine young piece that's just a bit too big for your needs, take it home, cut it into lumps as big as your thumb, put them in a jar and cover them with sherry. It will keep for months, and if you want to make a little ice cream or sliced apples or plain yogurt taste nice, add a few teaspoons of sherry. If you want a piece of ginger to cook with, fish it out of the jar, slice it and treat it as if it were fresh. And if you have a cold, a glass of the lovely ginger-flavoured sherry is better than any prescription.

Best of all, learn to make ginger tea. Drink it cold in the summer and hot in the winter, particularly when you need to be warmed, stroked, cuddled or just plain reassured. Ginger tea is basically an Indonesian drink, usually taken very strong after dinner. I prefer to make it a little less fierce, but how you make it — how much you dilute it and what you choose to mix with it — is a matter of personal taste.

The basic recipe is four cups of water and a piece of ginger as long as your finger, grated into a saucepan. Add four tablespoons of brown sugar or honey, half a lemon and four cloves. Bring it to a boil, then simmer it, covered, for 15 minutes. Strain and drink it hot, or leave it to cool and then strain it into a jug to keep in the fridge. Diluted with soda water, ginger tea is better than any ginger ale, mixed with whiskey it's a famous drink called Whiskey Mac, with a little gin it's very refreshing and with some slices of fruit it's a great punch. There is no end to the versatility of ginger tea . . . or for that matter, to ginger itself, now that you know how to cook with it.

FISH AND GINGER

Salmon, cod, halibut or trout
a thumbsized piece of fresh ginger, cut into matchstick strips
flour

Fry the ginger in a little oil. Flour the fish and fry with the ginger for no more than 8 minutes per inch of thickness, turning just once.

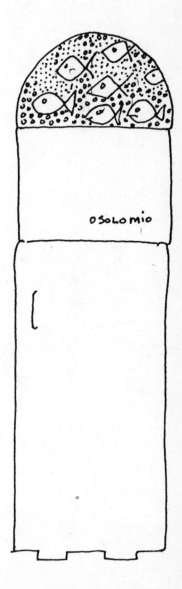

One Potato, Two Potato, Three Potato, More!

Celebrating the Feast of New Potatoes.

One sunny June morning in Tokyo, in a little street wide enough for four to walk abreast, my neighbour got up early. Almost everybody in Tokyo gets up early; there are trains to catch, sidewalks to sweep and the market, that fragile garden of money, to prune and cultivate. Tokyo in the early morning is concentrated business. There is no city anywhere more crowded, and it is a beehive in springtime.

But Tokyo is a city of contrasts. There are 10-lane highways downtown needing bridges to cross them, and there are lanes in which a bicycle (the man who sells noodles rides a bicycle and pulls a trailer behind) is almost too big. Outside major office buildings fortune-tellers still sit, tucked into corners on stools, and expensive suits with computers in their briefcases stop for palm readings, the real low-tech truth, before ramming themselves back into high gear for the rest of the race.

Dinner can cost you $300. Or if you know where and how to look for it, it can still cost $5. Little old women, frail as mice in brown kimonos, walk quietly alongside energetic girls in the latest fashions. But in the subway, where 200 people try to cram into space for 100, the mice become tigers, with elbows and ruthlessness far beyond that of any NHL enforcer.

Tokyo is a city of contrasts. My neighbour, who got up earlier than usual, was tending his strawberry plant — one plant in a pot, watered and fertilized daily, moved hourly to get the maximum sun and snipped, pruned and groomed more carefully than a bonzai tree. It had exactly five strawberries. There was nothing else growing in his house but every morning at first sun he was a gardener, long before he was a *sarari*, a dark suit in an office of dark suits.

This particular morning was special. It was time to harvest the strawberries, all five of them, one apiece for his wife, three children and him, the gardener, the horticulturist, the back-to-earth provider of good things.

He took the day off. Somebody in the office understood that it was necessary, that it was a personal festival, and the children stayed home from school for the same reason. They admired the bush in the early sunlight and they admired it at hourly intervals, until the fruits were at their warmest. And then, in an intensity of pleasure, anticipation of fulfillment, in their best clothes, the neighbour, with a small pair of scissors, chose a strawberry for his wife, who bowed, and one each for his children, who also bowed. Then, with the reverence of wine experts, savouring every drop of juice, every texture, they ate them. And bowed again.

This column is really about new potatoes, which are not — or *ought* not to be — very different from strawberries. For a month they will be in the stores and the gardens of the lucky. We can't all take a day off for the first digging ("Dear Miss Robinson: Sean can't come to school today because we are eating new potatoes"), but we can all have private festivals and get the most out of a seasonal crop. The little new potatoes have a taste and a texture that won't freeze and won't keep. They come once a year, and they don't get the press and the hype that strawberries do because they're just potatoes and potatoes, because they're cheap and basic and sort of dirty, never get very high on the gourmet's Top 40.

But new potatoes — let's go back to the man in Tokyo. Suppose we get up one day, have breakfast, take a deep breath, look at the sky instead of watching the weatherman and decide that today is the day of the Feast of New Potatoes. There is no official proclamation; this is just the day when we celebrate the dirt and the earth and the farmers and the cows who make the milk that makes the butter, and it can be any day you choose, sun or rain, indoors or outdoors, house or apartment, one people, two, three or a crowd.

You can drive (or bus, or walk or cycle) to a farm or a store or a roadside stand. You can take kids, dogs, your spouse or even a first date to participate in the Great Process of Selecting the New Potatoes. Of course, you pick them over. You want each of them to be exactly the same size. Some like them small, some like them medium, but if all the potatoes are the same size they will all take exactly the same time to cook, so you choose each one with the same care and concern as you do when you buy clothes. Two people's worth of new potatoes will cost you a dollar.

But it's not the money that makes a festival, it's the concern and the dedication. Take them home. Don't leave them twist-topped in a plastic bag — they need to breathe. Don't put them in the fridge for a week; they are a spring and early summer vegetable, the first things to push themselves out of the dark and cold of winter, and they don't like going back to it. Take them home to eat that evening, take a steak if you need it, or even better, some lamb chops, but concentrate on the potatoes. When I lived in Ireland we would try to shoot a rabbit for supper, but if we didn't nobody really minded, because the main focus of the meal was an enormous pot of potatoes cooked on the

NEW POTATOES

new potatoes
large pot of water
4 - 5 stalks mint
1 tbsp salt

Bring the water to a rolling boil, throw in the salt and mint and then the potatoes. Cover and cook for 14 - 15 minutes. Drain, replace the lid and allow to sit in their own steam for a minute. Serve with butter, some freshly ground black pepper and a good handful of chopped parsley.

FRENCH-STYLE

Deep-fry the very small new potatoes until they're light brown and then roll them in powdered sugar.

JAPANESE-STYLE

Steam the new potatoes with soy sauce and sake.

CHINESE-STYLE

Boil the new potatoes in hot pots with thick hunks of very fat, very salty pork.

fire, drained outside the front door and tipped, steaming, onto the kitchen table.

There is the mint to find. Most gardeners have more mint than they want, and during the summer it is in most supermarkets. It's another enormous expenditure — 45, even 50 cents — but this is a festival as important as Thanksgiving, so be reckless: spend the money and take home your bunch of mint.

Kids raised on French fries from McBurger may not understand the importance of new potatoes for supper. But they will if you create the atmosphere. Christmas is a festival of anticipation, and anticipation is a manufactured product. Everybody has (or wishes he or she had) a grandmother who lived on the Prairies or on a farm, surviving long, hard winters and even longer, harder poverty on a diet of potatoes. These stories are much more effective than "When I was a kid I had two paper routes," so tell them. Lie if you have to; this is mythology you're dealing with.

"New potatoes for supper....
And we don't have to peel them; we just rub them with our thumbs under running water, leaving some of the curly, thin skin."

"New potatoes for supper....
Shall we steam them or boil them?"

"New potatoes for supper....
D'you think they'd look nice on the turkey plate?" If you do it right, this could be the most inexpensive and the most rewarding party you've ever had, and next year the kids will be reminding you. There *are* fussy things you can do with new potatoes. The French deep-fry the very small ones until they're light brown and then roll them in powdered sugar. The Japanese pick mountain potatoes and steam they with soy sauce and sake, and the Chinese put them in hot pots with thick hunks of very fat, very salty pork. But I am a purist. I steam them or I boil them. Boiling requires a large pot, the water brought to a rolling boil, four or five stalks of mint and a tablespoon of salt thrown in and then the potatoes, which cook covered over high heat for 14 to 15 minutes. Don't poke them all with a knife; they need to stay whole to cook properly. Drain off the water, put the lid back on and let them sit in their own steam for a minute while you set out the plates, a large dish of butter, some freshly ground pepper and maybe a good handful of chopped parsley all over butter where everybody can reach it and it's each for him or herself to split the potatoes, dab on an excessive amount of butter and maybe a little salt and eat them when they're still a little too hot for comfort. Like Christmas, this is not a time to be concerned with calories. This is self-indulgence, this is basic religion, a feast and a festival. *Enjoy!*

And you *could* bow.

A Flash In The Pan

Fish is quick, easy and best when it's fresh.

Fish is one of the easiest and most expressive words to say in sign language. Thumb up, fingers together, your hand pointed the same way as your feet, you bend your wrist in a sideways wave, putting as much wiggle into it as you can. That's fish — *all* fish, every live, jumping wriggler that ever swam in the sea. It's a joyous sign, very hard to do without smiling.

The sign for pleasure is the same hand, thumb up and fingers together, covering your belly button. Now move it round and round, in the simple old expression of content that we all use after a good dinner. That's the sign for pleasure — *all* pleasure, every good thing that happens to any one of your five senses and any other unexplainable comfortable, warm, exciting thing, physical or emotional.

Spoken words are not so general. They either complicate pleasures — over-sophisticate them — or oversimplify them. Either way, they diminish them, particularly with food. "We eat gourmet on weekends," said a student at one of my cooking classes, "but just ordinary all week. I don't want to be bothered." She came wanting to learn something complicated, and when she found it was easy she was disappointed, because she thought her friends wouldn't be impressed by anything that wasn't difficult. She needed to be bothered, and just wasn't prepared to think simple, to rub her belly and smile at some small delight.

So many of us are scared, or haven't learned how to be really appreciative, of things which are ridiculously simple . . . like fish. Most of us know how to barbecue or stuff and bake a salmon (although even that can be complicated by people who invent techniques for wrapping it in foil and running it through two complete sani-cycles of the dishwasher) because salmon quite deservedly, has a high-society reputation. Like steak, it's obviously the best. Nobody who is fed salmon can feel in any way shortchanged.

Even more, it's part of the West Coast myth. All Canadians know that West Coast life is easy, that we don't work but just lie beside the sea on our five-day weekends, waiting for coho to swim into our hands.

POACHED SKATE

skate
2 cloves
1 tsp salt
a large strip orange peel
salt and pepper

Put the skate, cloves, orange peel and salt into a large pot of boiling water. Simmer for 10 minutes, drain and top the skate with a good daub of butter and a good sprinkle of pepper.

FISHCAKES

cold, mashed potato
equal amount of cold, cooked fish (or canned tuna)
1 medium onion, finely chopped
1 egg
a handful of chopped parsley
salt and pepper
breadcrumbs or flour

Mix all the ingredients together vigorously and roll into balls as large as eggs. Flatten each one into a round cake as thick as your finger. Pat breadcrumbs or flour onto each side and fry them crisp and brown over medium heat. Eat with ketchup or Worcestershire sauce.

FISHCAKES CREOLE

Make as for Fishcakes and substitute cornmeal for the flour or breadcrumbs and add a little cayenne pepper.

FISH PIE

Mix all the ingredients together as for Fishcakes then place the mixture in a buttered pie dish, brush butter over the top and bake at 350°F for 45 minutes.

BARBECUED SALMON FILLETS

salmon fillets
2 tbsp olive oil
1/2 tsp pepper
a good handful thyme,
tarragon or oregano
lemon juice

Marinate the salmon fillets in the olive oil, thyme and pepper. Leave for 1 hour, turning occasionally. Don't use salt. Grill the fish over hot coals, turning just once, and serve sprinkled with lemon juice.

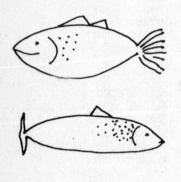

But fish in its other incarnations we have not yet fully accepted. Ling cod, snapper, skate wings, perch, rock cod . . . they're all swimming out there in the sea, and more and more of them are coming into the fish markets — nice, fresh, local fish for two dollars and change per pound.

The first thing to do with any fish you don't actually catch is buy it. And that is a simple art. The fish should *look* healthy — as shiny and firm as the deltoids on a muscle builder — and, most important, it should not smell fishy, not if it's fresh. A plastic tray of limp, grey fish hidden under two layers of saran wrap is not what you buy. Neither is anything that reminds you of the bucket the kids left in the trunk last time you went to the beach. Fresh fish is just that: fresh.

Take skate, which recently hit the New York scene as the "in" fish of the year. Skate is a different kind of fish because it doesn't have bones, which makes it very easy for beginners to deal with. Skate is actually the wing of a big fish called a ray, and in the middle of the wing is cartilage. When the fish is cooked, the meat is easily scraped from the cartilage. I put this cartilage in the blender with a clove of garlic and then feed it to the cat, but you can make fish stock of it if you have the inclination.

The simplest way to cook skate is to poach it in a good big pot of boiling water with two whole cloves, a large strip of orange peel and a teaspoon of salt. Simmer it for 10 minutes, then drain and top it with a daub of butter and a good sprinkle of pepper. Eat it immediately with boiled potatoes and fresh peas. Very simple, very comforting.

If you are sensible, you will buy a lot when the skate is fresh. You won't keep half of it in the fridge for a week; you'll cook it all at once and keep what you don't eat for next day, when you will make fishcakes. You'll need equal parts of cold mashed potatoes and cold fish, vigorously mixed together with a fork (the food processor makes it too smooth; fish cakes need texture), a finely chopped medium onion, a handful of chopped parsley and an egg. Make balls as big as a large egg, and on a board sprinkled with flour, flatten each ball into a round cake as thick as your little finger. Turn over to flour the other side, then fry both sides crisp and brown in a little vegetable oil over medium heat. Eat them with ketchup or Worcestershire sauce, for breakfast, supper or lunch.

If you want fish cakes Creole (very fashionable these days), use cornmeal instead of flour and add a little red cayenne pepper. And if you haven't got skate, use any cooked fish — cod, snapper, even canned salmon. Make little finger-sized fishcakes and serve them as party snacks, or don't make fishcakes at all — put the mixture in a buttered pie dish, brush butter over the top and bake at 350°F for 45 minutes. That's fish pie. Or put the mixture in a shallow pie plate, make four depressions in the top with a spoon and slide eggs in. Bake until the eggs are set and you have a *boudin de poisson aux oeufs,* which your kids in French immersion will call "that thing you make with eggs on top."

It's easy to be successful with fish. It's also easy to experiment with it. There's only one rule to successful fish cookery: don't overcook it. What's become known all over North America as the Canadian rule recommends 10 minutes per inch of thickness over high heat for any fish, baked, poached or grilled. Really fresh fish takes even less time, about eight minutes per inch.

Much of the wild, sea-going salmon will be barbecued. A whole salmon is dramatic, but it tastes better barbecued in pieces. Salmon can easily be dried out by hot coals, but you can avoid this by using a simple technique which produces a juicy, flavourful, moist piece of fish. Put a couple of tablespoons of olive oil in a dish with a good handful of thyme, oregano or tarragon. Add a half-teaspoon of pepper and turn the filets in the oil. Leave them for an hour, turning occasionally. Don't use salt; it will suck out the juices. Grill the fish over hot coals, turning just once, and serve sprinkled with lemon juice.

That's outdoor fish. Now for some indoor. Fancy restaurants offer *truite meunière,* which simply means trout in the style of the miller. What does the miller do? He grinds flour. So trout, salmon, cod or snapper can all be *meuniered* just by tossing them in flour. Toss four or five tablespoons of flour, a little pepper and whatever herb you choose into a big plastic bag. Add the fish, close the bag and turn the fish over and over to coat it all with flour. Fry the fish in a little oil over high heat for a maximum of 10 minutes per inch, turning it once, and serve immediately with lemon quarters. The flour seals in the flavours just as the oil did.

Then there's fish teriyaki. Cod, snapper, salmon and even little smelts go very well with this quick, almost authentic, Japanese style of cooking. Cut the fish into serving portions (except for smelts, which you leave whole), then put four tablespoons of vegetable oil, two tablespoons of soya sauce and one tablespoon of sugar into a cold frypan. Heat at medium until it bubbles, stirring occasionally, then lay in the fish. Cook 10 minutes per inch, turning once, top with a squeeze of lemon juice and serve immediately.

Fish is easy. And quick. And best when it's fresh.

BOUDIN DE POISSON AUX OEUFS

Mix all the ingredients together as for Fishcakes then put the mixture in a shallow pie plate, make four depressions in the top with a spoon and slide eggs in. Bake at 350°F until the eggs are set.

FISH MEUNIERE

trout, salmon, cod or snapper
4 - 5 tbsp flour
pepper
Thyme, marjoram, or tarragon, fresh or dry, just one not all.

Toss the fish in a bag with the flour, pepper and whichever herb you choose. Fry the fish in a little oil over high heat for a maximum of 10 minutes per inch of thickness. Turn once. Serve immediately with lemon quarters.

FISH TERIYAKI

cod, snapper, salmon or smelts
4 tbsp vegetable oil
2 tbsp soya sauce
1 tbsp sugar
lemon juice

Cut the fish into serving portions (except the smelts which you leave whole). Put the oil, soya sauce and sugar into a cold frypan and heat at medium heat until it bubbles, stirring occasionally. Lay in the fish and cook for 10 minutes per inch of thickness, turning once. Top with a squeeze of lemon juice and serve immediately.

Lend Me Your Ears

. . . and I'll tell you all there is to know about fresh corn.

When corn is in season and in all the supermarkets, corn authorities, the people who really *know* about corn, are tearing back its leaves and checking its insides to make sure they have the very best, very freshest cobs — corn better than anybody else's. Sometimes, because such energy is liberated by the idea of really fresh corn, squabbles and snatchings and elbowings are as fierce as ever happened at a $1.49 day.

These corn strippers, who have the serious, solemn faces of bargain hunters at flea markets, are the same people who go around pushing their thumbs into melons and avocados — which, incidentally, is not the way to check for ripeness. A ripe melon exudes a small perfume at the stem end, not very pronounced and not the sort of scent you might dab behind the ears, but a scent all the same — the honest smell of sun and summer, the flavour of God's smile, which is the same as the bouquet of good red wine. But the corn strippers and the melon pressers don't know that.

A bin of unripe avocados starts off the day with each and every avocado as hard as a baseball. By noon at least half of them have had a good workout with a dozen or so strong thumbs, and they *will* be soft, not because they're any riper, but because they have given up the struggle. They will be as bruised as novices at their first karate class, and whoever takes them home will be bitterly disappointed. Hard avocados are hard avocados, and they will ripen best if left to sleep overnight with a ripe banana in a paper bag. Melons, too for that matter. And since we are on the subject of melons — those lovely, ripe, warm, small Okanagan melons with flesh the dark orange colour of saffron and not the pales, hard, year-round bowling balls trucked in from far away — let's remember the Persians, who have always eaten melons, and sprinkle a healthy grinding of fresh, coarse black pepper over each slice before we slurp into it. We had this argument over strawberries: *"Pepper* on *strawberries?"* And then came the second response all raving about it. So try it now with melon, and see how the pepper brings out the flavour.

And if you're frying a bit of chicken, dusted with flour or breadcrumbs or just fried the way you like to fry it, when it's 10 minutes from being cooked put half an onion and a clove of garlic, both finely chopped, into the pan with a sprinkle of curry powder and a little salt. Stir it a bit and let it cook for a minute while you cut the rind off four thick slices of melon and dice the flesh into bits as big as sugar cubes. Stir the melon into the pot, put the lid on and cook over low heat for 15 minutes. During that 15 minutes you can cook some rice (with two or three whole cardamoms buried at the bottom of the pot) and stir the chicken occasionally. I like to put the rice around the outside of a big platter and the chicken in the middle, dusted with cinnamon and sprinkled with grated coconut. If you want to make a big deal out of it — a supper to impress — then two bananas, quartered, peeled and fried for two minutes in butter, can be very decorative. So can green peas cooked in four tablespoons of water with lid on tight. Roasted and crushed peanuts are nice sprinkled over it, and so is chopped parsley and even a coarsely grated carrot. Any or all of these make a colourful meal. Decorating a dish like this is more fun than doing a cake, and a lot less trouble, but you don't *have* to have all the fancies; simple chicken and melon is just as nice.

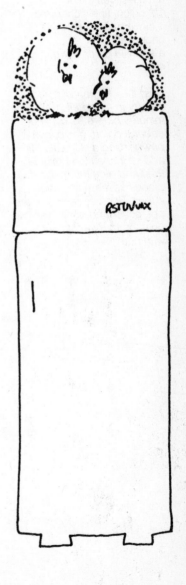

But we were taking corn home before we got sidetracked by melons, corn which we had chosen not by suspiciously stripping it, but by hefting in our hands and judging, with our farmer's intuition, whether it felt heavy for its size, whether it felt plump and comfortable just sitting there in our palms, sensing with our sixth sense (the Grandma sense that can unerringly proclaim, "That's a healthy baby!") that each cob we chose was the one somebody had been waiting a lifetime for. And besides, while everybody else was stripping, we got out of the parking lot.

Now there are folk myths about cutting corn in the garden and *running* not walking, with it to a pot of boiling water. Like all myths, it is something to believe in, something that might once have happened, and all it means is that corn should be eaten when it's fresh as possible. The best way to eat store-bought corn is to leave it in the husks until it's cooked. Boil it with the husk and silk on, adding a little more salt than usual to the water. Better yet, barbecue it. If it's really fresh, just throw it on the grill and turn it every two or three minutes. There is enough natural moisture in the cobs to steam them. The leaves (outside husks) will dry out and burn, but inside the corn will be slightly smoky, very sweet and just a little crunchy. If the corn is not fresh from the garden (or fresh off the roadside stand, with the tassels still wet), then soak it, the husks still on, in a bucket of water for an hour or two before barbecuing it. Whichever way you do it, *don't strip it back even a little bit;* leave the husks intact. They work better than aluminum foil, and they don't cost money.

Canned and frozen corn are available all year around. Both have their uses if there is no corn. A few kernels in the most ordinary of

CHICKEN AND CORN CHOWDER

1 can corn (creamed or whole kernel) or fresh corn scraped from the cob

Cook as for Chicken Chowder but substitute the corn for the 3 diced potatoes.
(see Page 89 for recipe)

CHICKEN AND MELON

1 Cut up chicken
4 thick slices melon
1/2 onion, finely chopped
1 clove garlic, finely chopped
a sprinkle curry powder
salt

Dust the chicken with flour and fry in a little oil. 10 minutes before it's cooked add the onion, garlic, curry powder and a little salt. Stir and let it cook for 1 minute. Peel and dice the melon into pieces as large as sugar cubes. Stir the melon into the pot, cover and cook over low heat for 15 minutes. Serve with rice.

soups will turn it into a chowder, because after 15 minutes of simmering, the natural starches come out and thicken the soup, while the natural sugars sweeten it. The combination of sugar and starch also permits you to use a bit more flavouring — an extra pinch of thyme or cayenne pepper, or a dash of vinegar — and you inevitably finish up with the kind of soup which people say, "I don't know how you do it, but you really make great soup."

Try this recipe for a chicken and corn chowder. Cut the kernels off eight cobs of fresh corn and, pressing hard with the back of a knife, scrape everything else off the cob — all the milky juices and scrappy little bits. Fry four slices of fatty side bacon (or a handful of bacon bits) in your big, heavy soup pot until the fat begins to run. Add one finely chopped large onion and cook for five minutes, stirring occasionally. Add a large grated carrot and the corn, juices and scrapings and all. Stir well, then add a cut-up chicken or about three pounds (one and a half kilograms) of chicken pieces. Stir well, add enough water to almost cover and bring to a boil. Add a little more pepper than you think wise, a teaspoon of green dill and a healthy pinch of red cayenne pepper. Cover and simmer for 25 minutes.

For a simple supper, serve immediately. For inexpensive luxury, add a few sliced mushrooms five minutes before serving. For fancy, stir in a cup of whipping cream. For pretty, sprinkle chopped parsley on top. For exotic, stir in a good teaspoon of curry powder with the onion. For your heart's sake, add a couple of cloves of garlic. For tomorrow, keep it in the refrigerator overnight.

And to become a family legend, teach your kids how to make it.

Liberation In The Kitchen

The best recipe for worry-free cookery is one that has no hard and fast rules.

The most widely used ingredient in North America is guilt. There's hardly a dish cooked without it. We go through recipes like astronauts at countdown, checking and double-checking: How many teaspoons in half a millilitre? How medium is an onion? And is a cup still a cup even if it's made of glass?

These are the small guilts, the little worries as basic to all kitchens as the kitchen sink. Butter is a medium guilt, along with extra-virgin olive oil ("Ours just says *virgin*. Will that be okay?) and room temperature (How do you take the temperature of a room? With a thermometer tucked under the carpet?).

Finally we get the really *big* guilts, like garlic. Somehow, we know that nobody eats it, despite the indisputable fact that 3,000 tons of it were sold in B.C. last year. So we sneak it into our cooking with our eyes closed, as though it were an accident ("My hand slipped!"). or an early symptom of Alzheimer's disease ("I thought you were my grandmother"). We don't talk about garlic any more than we talk about grandfather the bigamist.

Wine is a big guilt ("Will they know it had a screwtop?"), and from there things get worse and worse. Guilts of all shapes and sizes accumulate like odd socks in the laundry basket. The china's wrong, the salt isn't sea salt, the peppercorns don't come from Madagascar but from Kitchener, Ontario, and the pastry, the bread, the steak and even the tomatoes just don't look like they should. Neither do we. We look in the mirror, see we aren't centrefold material and feel guilty about it every minute until the guests go home.

Pretty soon this guilt becomes a habit, something to put on, like an apron, every time we go into the kitchen, and we look for ways to reinforce it, to starch it stiff. One of the most common and least recognized guilts is the kitchen work ethic. It simply says that if we haven't worked ourselves stupid, spent hours worrying about shopping for dinner and even more hours peeling, chopping, rolling, dicing, icing, stuffing, shaping and peering into the oven, dinner will be worthless, and our friends and families, those world renowned gourmets with palates more delicate than nightingales and taste buds

FISH SOUP (FOR 6)

2 lb fish, cut into serving
pieces
fish stock (see page 90,
Fish Chowder for recipe)
or substitute canned clam
juice diluted with water
2 medium onions, sliced
2 large or 4 medium
tomatoes, cut into eighths
6 tbsp olive oil
3 cloves garlic, unpeeled
thick slices of bread
juice of a lemon

*Heat the olive oil in a heavy
pan and stir in the onions
and the whole cloves of
garlic. Cook slowly until
transparent. Add the
tomatoes, stir and simmer
over medium/low heat. Strain
the fish stock into the pan,
add the fish and cook for a
maximum of 10 minutes.*

*Toast the bread and put a
slice in each serving bowl.
With a slotted spoon remove
the fish and lay it on the
bread. Stir the lemon juice
into the soup, then pour it
over the fish.*

as sensitive as the latest radar detectors, will *know*. And they will *tell*, branding us permanently as uncaring, incompetent and socially unacceptable cooks.

The truth is, most guests are simply grateful. They get a free dinner, with no dishes to wash, and the chance to go through your bathroom cupboard. They feel mildly guilty about things they don't think they should eat (like the aforementioned garlic), but as long as you don't *tell* them what they're eating, they can live with these things. That's what foreign names are all about. Nobody wants to eat snails, but everybody loves *escargots*. Liver is almost universally unpopular, but call it *foie gras* and you'll get rave reviews. Meat loaf is not acceptable, but the same ingredients called *pâté* bring compliments.

Take *bouillabaisse*, for which almost everyone has a recipe — a great, complicated, expensive formula calling for crab, mussels, clams, prawns, lobster, scallops and any other particularly expensive shellfish. It is usually a terrifying recipe, when the simple truth is bouillabaisse is no more (and no less) than fish stew, a dish made in a hurry by the wife of a fisherman who came home hungry with a few unsold fish in a bag over his shoulder.

In France, Italy, Hungary, Greece and even on the East Coast of Canada, fishing people know about this stew. And they all make it out of what's around. Sometimes they put wine in it, sometimes beer, sometimes just water. Sometimes five kinds of fish, sometimes three and sometimes one. They use whatever's handy and whatever's cheap. The expensive fish they sell.

On a fall evening, when it seems colder than it actually is because our systems still remember summer, there is nothing simpler, more filling or more cozy than a good fish soup. To feed six people you will need about two pounds of fish — *any* fish, as long as it's cheap — and about a pound of fish trimmings (bones, heads, fins — whatever the fish shop will give you). Put the trimmings in a big pot with a half-dozen peppercorns, a teaspoon of salt, a bay leaf and about eight cups of water. Bring to a boil and simmer for 30 minutes.

Meanwhile, slice two medium onions and cut two big or four medium tomatoes into eighths. Warm about six tablespoons of olive oil in a heavy stewing pot or casserole, then stir in the onions and three whole, unpeeled garlic cloves. Cook slowly until they are transparent. Add the tomatoes, stir and leave everything to melt together over medium-low heat. When the fish stock is ready, strain it onto the onions and tomatoes, add the fish (cut into serving pieces, not little nibbly bits) and cook for a maximum of 10 minutes.

Now toast thick slices of bread, get out six bowls and put a slice in each. With a slotted spoon, lift out the fish and lay it on the bread. Stir the juice of a lemon into the soup, then pour it over the fish. That's it — supper's ready. There are no hard and fast rules. Everything about fish soup is approximate, except for not overcooking the fish. Always make the stock first, then add the fish.

This recipe, which is basically Greek, can be made richer and bigger by adding *avgolemono,* a Greek egg/lemon sauce. Beat a couple of eggs, then slowly, while beating, add lemon juice until the mixture is smooth and frothy. Pour a couple of spoonfuls of hot stock into the egg mixture, then a couple more. Continue adding and beating until you have almost a cup. Now stir this sauce into the soup.

You can add two cups of cooked rice instead of using bread as long as you don't stir the fish pieces and break them up into mush. A little oregano tossed in with the onions and tomatoes is equally Greek, as is more garlic, or even thyme.

The Portuguese make a similar soup. They add three or four medium potatoes (don't peel them; just wash and cube them) and a bunch of coriander or chopped parsley. Sometimes they substitute wine for half of the water, and sometimes they add chopped red and green peppers and clams if they have them. Instead of toasted bread they use croutons (cubes of bread fried in olive oil over medium heat), and if they want to spice it up they add paprika. The Belgians make the same stew using butter instead of olive oil, and celery and sage leaves instead of the tomatoes.

If you can't find a fish shop with trimmings, use canned clam juice diluted with water. And if you're absolutely desperate, frozen fish will do as long as you add a little more salt and pepper and melt an anchovy fillet with the onions. If you want to be extravagant, beer makes a very rich stock. And if you want to be French, add a half-pound of mushrooms when you add the fish, and stir in a half-cup of sour cream just before serving. Sometimes I add a little plain, old Canadian rye to the sauce, and sometimes I don't. There are no rules, and a good fish soup is the first act of liberation in the kitchen, a giant step away from guilt.

GREEK-STYLE

Make Fish Soup and add Avgolemono Sauce (see page 87 for recipe) or some oregano or thyme and more garlic.

PORTUGUESE-STYLE

3 - 4 medium potatoes, washed and cubed
a bunch cilantro or parsley, chopped
1 red pepper, chopped
1 green pepper, chopped
clams (optional)
paprika
croutons

Make Fish Soup and add the potatoes, cilantro or parsley, some chopped pepper, clams and some paprika. Substitute wine for half of the water and use croutons instead of the slices of bread.

BELGIAN-STYLE

3 or 4 stalks celery
sage leaves
butter

Make Fish Soup but substitute butter for the olive oil, and celery and sage leaves for the tomatoes.

FRENCH-STYLE

1/2 lb mushrooms
1/2 cup sour cream

Make Fish Soup and when you add the fish, add the mushrooms and stir in the sour cream. A little rye can be added.

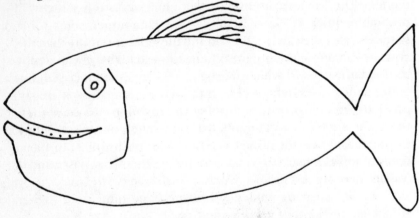

Full of Beans

Peasants and gourmets alike prize these nourishing, comforting, versatile little morsels.

TUSCAN BEAN SOUP

1/2 lb small, white beans
water
1 tsp salt
1/2 tsp black pepper
bay leaf
2 large cloves garlic, chopped
2 tbsp olive oil
a large handful of chopped parsley

Pour boiling water over the white beans and let them soak for 1 hour. Remove and cook them in 5 cups water, with no salt, and the bay leaf. Simmer over low heat for 1 1/2 hours with the lid three-quarters on the pot.

Remove half the amount of beans with a slotted spoon and whiz them in a food processor or blender. Add the pepper and salt and return the purée to the pan, adding a little more water if necessary. Reheat.

In another pan, cook the chopped, garlic cloves slowly in the olive oil until they change colour. Stir them and the oil into the soup along with the parsley.

In the tombs of the ancient Egyptians, alongside the pharaohs — the kings of all kings, who were buried with their gold, jewels, silks, soldiers, wives, women and slaves — there were pots of the things they thought most precious, things which they considered essential if heaven was to compare in any way with the splendour of their earthly lives.

There were things beside their mummified royalty which have now become household words for precious: myrrh and frankincense, essential oils for expensive perfumes, saffron and even garlic. There were weapons and mirrors, bobby pins and drinking cups, eating bowls and wine bottles — much the same sort of stuff the rich and famous take on picnics today.

And among all these fancy, expensive things, there were jars of beans — not preserved green beans from France with gourmet labels, but plain and simple dried beans, the kind that are so cheap in any market or corner store, and which, largely because they *are* so cheap, are so sadly neglected in most North American cooking.

The baked beans of Quebec were gently cooked for hours with pork and maple syrup, but they fell victim to the craze for saving time, and sad imitations of them were stuffed into cans for quick and easy dinners. The canners discovered that chili was another highly profitable, quick and easy item — some hamburger, some tomato sauce and a lot of beans . . . the can and the label cost more than the contents. Beans suddenly meant cheap — actually, cheap and nasty, the food of last resort which, like beer, has very little social standing.

But almost everywhere else in the world, dried beans are still precious. French gourmets drool at the mention of a *cassoulet* and there are three-star restaurants that owe much of their reputations to such basic peasant dishes as lentils and mushrooms. In Italian households, kids learn to cook beans before they learn pasta, and in Naples there are restaurants which specialize in *pasta fagioli,* a lovely, rich, warm, satisfying winter dish made of nothing more than pasta — almost any kind of pasta — and beans.

In Yugoslavia there are wonderful bean soups with smoked sausage.

In Mexico and Guatemala there are infinite variations of beans and rice, and in Romania there is a fall and winter country soup called *ciorba de fasole,* which is thick, nourishing and satisfying, and uses very little meat. The Spaniards, the Austrians, the Scots and the Brits ... they all make bean dishes.

All good bean recipes come from the countryside, and they all have the same two things in common: beans and a long cooking time — two, four or six hours. We tend to confuse long *cooking* times with long *working* times, while the truth of the matter is that country folk probably have less time to spend getting dinner ready than their city brethren.

Peasant women are always pictured puttering about in the kitchen baking pies. What *really* happened was that dinner went on the stove to cook itself while the women washed, darned, milked, raised babies, plucked chickens, salted meat, swept, scrubbed, doctored, comforted, counselled and frequently, as you can see in photographs in the Saskatchewan archives, pulled plows. In one picture, four women in frilly-front blouses and big, floppy hats, with ropes over their shoulders, drag a plow steered by one of their husbands. The other three men are busy building a house. Those women also had to go home and get supper, without too much time and certainly without too much cash — which is where beans come in.

Good, simple, easy food, beans need very little preparation time. They spend their time from then on perfuming the house with a rich, wonderful, somebody-lives-here fragrance, while you either do nothing or enjoy the kids, teach the dog to sing or yourself to knit. Beans are not only easy, they are nourishing and comforting, and once you know the rules, they are versatile — for good times, hard times, company or family.

Fava beans, white beans, navy beans, red beans, lima beans or, if you want to be fancy, the little green *flageolots* from France, which are the champagne of beans — they are all initially treated the same. Soaking them all night produces a mild (but pleasant and bitter-tasting) fermentation. So instead of doing that, pour boiling water over them and let them soak for an hour before cooking. Never salt beans, no matter what the recipes say, until they are at least half cooked; salt makes them tough. The third rule is that beans need flavour — not the fake flavours of garlic salt or Old Mother Whatsit's Genuine Italian Taste Sensation Powder, but the honest, genuine, simple flavours that come from either olive oil or butter. That's all you really need to know.

The simplest of all bean dishes is Tuscan bean soup. The Tuscans grow Chianti, make cheeses from buffalo milk and cook the best food in Italy. Pour boiling water over a half-pound of small white beans and let them soak for an hour. You don't have to stand and watch them, and if it runs to two hours, nobody will know but you. Cook them

BEAN SOUP FRENCH-STYLE

3 potatoes, diced
salt and pepper
1 onion, chopped
1/2 cup cream
croutons

Follow the recipe for Tuscan Bean Soup and add the potatoes and some extra salt and pepper to the boiling beans. Blend or process the whole thing, and fry the onion with the garlic. Stir in the cream and serve with croutons and parsley.

RICH BEAN SOUP

3 - 4 cups chicken or turkey stock
1/2 tsp grated nutmeg
1/2 cup cream
2 stalks celery, sliced paper-thin

Boil the beans as for Tuscan Bean Soup but allow the water to almost boil away, then add the chicken or turkey stock. Stir in the nutmeg and cream and at the last moment add the celery. Serve while the celery is still crunchy.

BEANS AS AN ITALIAN VEGETABLE

3 tbsp good olive oil
1 onion, finely chopped
1 clove garlic, finely chopped
1 tomato, finely chopped
salt and pepper
1/2 tsp dried oregano

Boil the beans as for Tuscan Bean Soup and allow the water to boil down to within a quarter of an inch at the bottom. Stir in the oil, onion, garlic, tomato and seasonings. Stir well and serve hot or cold.

PEASANT BEANS

1/2 smoked garlic sausage, sliced
2 tomatoes, finely chopped

Make as for Beans as a Vegetable and add the smoked garlic sausage and tomatoes. You can substitute 2 smoked pork hocks or 1 smoked pork jowl for the garlic sausage.

in about five cups of fresh water with no salt, just a bay leaf. Let them simmer over very low heat for an hour and a half, with the lid three-quarters on the pot.

Take out half of the beans with a slotted spoon and mash or whizz them a minute in the food processor or blender. Add a really good sprinkling (at least a half teaspoon) of black pepper and a teaspoon of salt. Add the purée to the whole beans and, if needed, a little more water to get a thick, soupy consistency. Reheat. Meanwhile, chop two large garlic cloves (no garlic presses; chop them with a knife) and cook them slowly over low heat in two tablespoons of olive oil until they change colour and smell nutty. Stir them and the oil into the soup, along with a large handful of finely chopped parsley. That's it. Soup's on, the simplest of all classic bean recipes.

If six extra people arrive for supper, dice three potatoes and add them and some extra salt and pepper to the boiling beans. Blend or process the whole thing, and fry a chopped onion with the garlic. Serve it with croutons and a good sprinkling of finely chopped parsley, and if you want to be extravagant, stir in a half cup of cream. That's a French-style bean soup.

To make a really rich soup, let the water in which the beans are cooked almost boil away, then add three or four cups of chicken or turkey stock. Stir in a half teaspoon of grated nutmeg with a half cup of cream, and at the very last moment add two stalks of celery, sliced paper-thin. Serve while the celery is still crunchy. If you have to wait for people to come to the table, don't add the celery until they are actually sitting there, looking hungry.

Half a smoked garlic sausage and three chopped tomatoes added with the garlic and onions will turn your beans into a basic, all-purpose peasant dish, as will a couple of smoked pork hocks or a smoked pork jowl.

Plainly cooked beans (simmered until they're done — no salt, no nothing — and the water boiled down until there's about a quarter-inch left on the bottom of the pan) are miraculously transformed by stirring in three tablespoons of good olive oil and one onion, one tomato (seeds and all) and one clove of garlic, all of them finely chopped. Add pepper and salt and a half teaspoon of dried oregano. Stir well and eat hot as a vegetable, or cold next day as an appetizer. On the third day, add a little water to what's left over, bring to a boil and mash — instant bean soup.

Cooking beans is like one-finger piano playing: a little practice, and you can make yourself very happy.

An Apple a Day Keeps The Boredom Away

Expanding your apple recipe repertoire.

If you want to become enormously unpopular with the neighbourhood kids, you will open the door at Halloween and be shocked ("My goodness, it's a witch!"), amused ("Hey, Chuck, come and see this one!") and finally generous: "Here's a nice, red apple."

Some kids, with 300 pounds of candy already in their pillowcases, look at you with pity. "Haven't you got any candy?" asked one particularly nice child, and when I said, "No," he offered me some: "I've got lots." But most kids, despite the 300 pounds of sugar they already have, react to apples with a mixture of stunned disbelief and outright scorn, unable to decide whether you have no money or no imagination.

I can understand this reaction in the country, where apples actually grow on trees and normal kids know the best places to pick them for free. But in urban circles, where red, green and yellow apples flourish only in supermarkets, I would hope that a fine, fresh, juicy, rosy apple would be as desirable as the first strawberries, a special pleasure and a seasonal treat, instead of a reluctant duty born of the half-remembered adage, "An apple a day keeps the doctor away."

Apples in lunchboxes, apples in pies and apples in applesauce... that seems to be the extent of most people's apple repertoire. Apple juice comes in bottles, and apple leather from the health food stores gets taken skiing. But the old recipes, the farmhouse recipes, don't get much action, not even when apples are only 39 cents a pound.

Breakfast is as good a place to start as any. Fry a few strips of bacon until they're almost crisp, then push them to one side and fry slices of apple in the bacon fat. Turn them once, let them get slightly brown (if they go transparent first then take them out before they go brown; some apples cook differently than others), sprinkle them with a little cinnamon and eat them with the bacon. Half sweet, half tart, spicy with the cinnamon, slightly juicy and richly flavoured with the bacon, fried apples are addictive. I buy bacon ends (some stores and delis call them off-cuts) for 50 cents a pound, just scraps of bacon and ham, and I fry them until the fat and the flavour come out. Then I cook the apples, which taste exactly the same as they do with the expensive

PORK CHOP AND APPLE STEW

4 pork chops
1 medium onion, thinly sliced
2 apples, cored and sliced crosswise
oil
cinnamon
1 cup apple juice or cider
1 bay leaf
1 tsp salt
1 tsp dried basil or thyme
cheese

Brown the chops quickly over high heat in a little oil. Add the onion and fry over medium heat. Remove the meat and onions from the pan and keep warm. Add some more oil and fry the apples until they're light brown. Dust with cinnamon. Layer the apples, meat and onions in a casserole, baking dish or frypan. Add the apple juice or cider, bay leaf, salt and basil or thyme. Bake for 45 minutes with the lid on tight. Then cover with cheese and broil until brown and bubbly.

PORK AND APPLE CASSEROLE

2 lb stewing pork, cubed
2 medium onions, sliced
2 green apples, cored and cut into chunks
4 oz mushrooms
1 tsp rosemary
1 tsp pepper
juice of half a lemon
1 cup dry cider or apple juice

Dust the meat with flour and quickly brown it, a few cubes at a time, in a casserole. Remove the meat, add the onions and slightly brown them. Add the rosemary, pepper, lemon juice and the cider or apple juice.

Add more liquid if necessary (the meat should be not quite covered). Cover and cook in a 400°F oven for 15 - 20 minutes. Turn the oven to 275°F and cook for 1 1/2 hours longer. Add the mushrooms and apples after 1 hour, stir, cover and continue cooking.

bacon except for the added pleasure of knowing that I have been smart.

Apples and pork go particularly well together. In the same way that such things as strawberries and cream, bacon and eggs and fish and chips were made for each other, so were pigs and orchards. Way back in history, before cookbooks, before turkeys and certainly before *Gourmet* magazine, whole pigs were roasted on spits for fall feasts, along with apples on long sticks, held over the fire and under the drippings for the last half hour, until the whole village was ready to be fed.

I still prefer pork to turkey, and I always put whole, unpeeled, medium-sized onions alongside the roast in the pan for the last hour of cooking. Then for the last half hour I put in apples. I core them and, to keep them from bursting, either peel the top half of each or carefully cut a line through the peel around the middle. I baste the apples once or twice with the pan juices, then serve them whole alongside the pork.

Apples cooked the same way are quite extraordinary with roast duck — the slight acidity of the juices makes a very light, digestible gravy. Quartered and cored apples, cut into good-sized chunks, tossed in lemon juice and then sprinkled with cinnamon, pepper and salt, make a wonderful, simple stuffing for roast chicken.

But you don't have to turn on the oven to cook the apples. A frypan with a lid, two big pork chops, two or three apples and a thinly sliced onion make a very good stovetop casserole for two people. Brown the pork chops quickly in a spoonful of oil, then push them aside and lightly fry the onion. Push the onion aside (or take it out if the pan gets crowded) and lightly fry the apples, which you have sliced as thick as your finger. Now rearrange everything: the onions on the bottom, then some slices of apple, then the chops and finally the remaining apple. Add a teaspoon of basil, tarragon or thyme, a little pepper or salt and a cup of apple juice. Bring to a boil with the lid off, then simmer, covered, for 30 minutes. With rice, potatoes or, best of all, heavy rye bread, this is a wonderful winter dinner. If you don't have apple juice, cider is fine, and if you *do* have apple juice but want to get the taste of Normandy, add a shot of rye (that's right, plain old Canadian rye) with the apple juice.

For an easy and economical casserole, the sort of thing you make for Saturday supper when the family has been out all day getting hungry, two pounds of stewing pork will go a long way with apples. The cheapest way to buy it is to get a chunk of shoulder and cut it into cubes yourself. Dust the meat with a little flour and quickly brown it, a few cubes at a time, in the bottom of a casserole. Remove the meat, add two good-sized sliced onions and lightly brown them, then add a teaspoon of rosemary, about a teaspoon of pepper (no salt), the juice of half a lemon and a cup of dry cider or apple juice.

The meat should just be poking up through the liquid, not quite covered. Add more liquid if necessary, but remember that the juices will come out of the meat and the onions, so less liquid means more flavour. Cover and cook in a 400°F oven for 15 to 20 minutes. Turn the oven to low (275°F) and cook for an hour and a half more. After an hour (30 minutes before you eat), add four ounces of sliced mushrooms and two green apples, cored and cut into chunks. Stir once, put the lid back on and remark on how nice the kitchen smells. If your family is late for supper, two hours of cooking won't hurt it at all.

When you get around to cooking a turkey (or even better, a goose), onions, sage and apples make a very simple stuffing with a taste that accentuates the richness of the bird and at the same time, because of the apples, counteracts any greasiness. Peel, core and coarsely chop six green apples. Toss them in a half-cup of rum and let them soak for three or four hours. Finely chop a large onion and mix it with the apples. Add about 12 ounces of fresh (not dry) breadcrumbs and a half-teaspoon of dried sage (or four or five fresh leaves, finely chopped). Mix well and stuff it into the bird's back end. If there's any left over, put it in the front end. Before taking the bird out of the pan, tilt it so the juices run out and flavour the gravy.

Finally, there's the simple baked apple, which to my mind is better than any complicated dessert and a fitting end to any fall or winter feast. Since the oven is on and already hot from cooking the main dish, have the apples ready and put them in to cook when everything else comes out. You'll need an apple corer, which costs about a dollar. The trick is to core to within a half-inch of the bottom of the apple. Pull out the corer and cut out the core with a small knife, leaving the bottom of the apple intact. Fill the cavity with brown sugar that's slightly moistened with lemon juice. Put the apples in a baking dish and cook at 350°F for 30 to 45 minutes and serve with a little thick cream poured over each plate.

APPLE, ONION AND SAGE STUFFING

6 green apples, peeled, cored and coarsely chopped
1/2 cup rum
1 large onion, finely chopped
12 oz fresh breadcrumbs
1/2 tsp dried sage (or 5 fresh leaves, finely chopped)

Toss the apples in the rum and let them soak for 3 - 4 hours. Mix in the onions, breadcrumbs and sage. Mix well and stuff into the bird's back end.

BAKED APPLE

apples (1 per person)
brown sugar
lemon juice

Core the apple, with an apple corer, to within half an inch of the bottom of the apple. Cut out the core with a small knife leaving the bottom of the apple intact. Fill the cavity with the sugar, slightly moistened with lemon juice. Place in a baking dish and cook at 350°F for 30 - 45 minutes. Serve with a little thick cream poured over the plate.

FRIED BACON AND APPLES

a few strips bacon
2 apples, sliced crosswise
cinnamon

Fry the bacon until almost crisp, push to one side and fry the apple slices. Turn them once and let them get slightly brown. Sprinkle with a little cinnamon and eat with the bacon.

Milk Made Portable

Reacquaint yourself with the simple, unavoidable virtue of cheese.

SAUCE MORNAY

1 oz butter
1 oz flour
1 cup milk
1/2 cup vegetable water
3 oz grated cheese, cheddar or gruyere
1/2 cup heavy cream (or 1/4 cup milk)
3 - 4 pinches of grated nutmeg
a good sprinkle of ground pepper
1/2 tsp salt

Melt the butter in a heavy saucepan, then stir in the flour over a low heat for 2 - 3 minutes. Combine the milk and vegetable water and heat without boiling. Remove the butter and flour from the heat and add the milk and stock and whisk it smooth. Replace the pan over low heat and cook for 1 - 2 minutes, stirring until the sauce thickens.

Stir in the heavy cream (or milk), remove the pan from the heat and stir in the cheese, pepper, nutmeg and salt.

MACARONI AND CHEESE

See Page 56 for recipe.

Every year the Dairy Bureau of Canada puts on a big, lavish competition for professional chefs, flying in contestants from all over Canada, putting them up in fancy hotels, providing them with fancy working conditions and finally, at an extraordinarily fancy banquet, giving fancy prizes to the winners. There are medals, of course, because chefs are as big on medals as Olympic athletes and Argentinian generals, but fancy prizes too, like trips for two around the world, all expenses paid.

And the whole contest is about cheese, cheese in anything and everything. Fish, meat, vegetables, desserts, soups, salads — so long as there's cheese in it, the Dairy Bureau is interested, because cheese is milk made portable, better than canned, powdered or irradiated milk, and nine times out of 10 it actually improves with age.

But why all the fuss? We all have a couple of cheese recipes in our kitchen vocabularies, all the way from "Dick and Jane Make Kraft Dinner" to *soufflé trois fromages.* We've all heard about brie and parmesan and double Gloucester, those fancy names in the gourmet magazines, but Canadian cheese suffers from the same problem as Canadian wine: if we can pronounce it, we think it can't be much good, so it always seems to be mentioned in an apologetic fashion, as though all really *good* food has to be imported.

There was a time when there wasn't much Canadian cheese, and it was easy to fall into the Velveeta habit. But today more than 100 different cheeses are made in Canada, and in every province, more and more farmers are moving into what was once considered a cottage industry for hippies with goats — or, at best, a quaint Mennonite habit.

Canadian cheese gets mentioned in European cookbooks. Canadian cheddar is spoken of respectfully as an alternative to English Cheshire, and brie from Quebec is noted for being different than brie from France, but a cheese worth eating.

Canadians, however, still treat cheese as either a foreign habit for special occasions or a quick lunchbox item. There's nothing in-between, and certainly cheese is not something to be regularly incorporated into daily cooking habits.

So let's talk about simplicities, like hearty slabs of oven-warmed bread, thick slices of cheese — cheddar, of course — and a Kentish onion salad. Cut a large onion into the thinnest rings you can manage; a serrated bread knife offers the quickest route. Liberally sprinkle the separated rings with black pepper, pour a half-cup of malt vinegar over them and let them sit for an hour or two. Then drain off the vinegar and eat the onions in large, indigestible bites. They will be crisp and sharp, the cheese smooth and sticky and the bread soft, warm and chewy. It's a wonderful meal for watching TV football, although it was first introduced to me by the old men who rowed the famous lifeboat of Walmer, a village in England. They ate it with large mugs of Kentish ale at their weekly suppers for the crew.

That's the simplest. Then comes cauliflower and cheese, easy to make *and* highly instructive in the two basic cooking processes of cheese. Cauliflower is cheap in winter, so start with a good, big cauliflower separated into bite-sized florets. Drop them into boiling, salted water for five minutes, then drain through a sieve, keeping the cooking liquid.

Now make a cheese sauce — *sauce Mornay,* if you want to be French-immersioned and keep up with your kids. Melt one ounce of butter in a heavy saucepan, then stir in one ounce of flour over low heat. Stir well for two to three minutes. Combine a half-cup of the vegetable water with one cup of milk, and heat without boiling. Remove the butter and flour from the heat, add the milk and vegetable stock (all in one go) and whisk it smooth. Put the pan back over low heat and cook for a minute or two, stirring with a wooden spoon until the sauce thickens.

If you want it to be wonderfully rich, stir in a half-cup of heavy cream; if not, use a quarter-cup of milk. Take the pan off the heat and stir in three ounces of grated gruyere, cheddar or any other firm (even old) cheese you have in the fridge, with a good sprinkling of ground pepper, three or four generous pinches of ground nutmeg and a half-teaspoon of salt. Butter a casserole, sprinkle a clove of chopped garlic over the bottom, put in the cauliflower, pour the Mornay sauce over it and shake it all down a little. Mix a quarter-cup of breadcrumbs with the same amount of grated cheese, sprinkle over top and then bake in a hot oven (200°C/400°F) for 15 to 20 minutes, until the top is golden brown.

That, in simple terms, is what fancy chefs call a *gratin* — you make a sauce, cook some vegetables, then cook the two together in the oven. The more cheese you put on top, the crustier it will get, and as you come to appreciate the flavour of the nutmeg, you will start to add additional spices, like cayenne pepper. You will start to use white wine instead of vegetable water. You will add leeks, boiled for five minutes and sliced. You will substitute fish for the cauliflower. You will discover

CAULIFLOWER CHEESE OR CAULIFLOWER AU GRATIN

1 large cauliflower, separated into florets
1/4 cup breadcrumbs
1/4 cup grated cheese
1 clove garlic, chopped
sauce mornay

Drop the cauliflower florets into boiling, salted water for 5 minutes and drain (use the stock in the sauce mornay).

Butter a casserole, sprinkle the garlic over the bottom, put in the cauliflower, pour over the sauce mornay (see above) and shake it all down a little. Mix the breadcrumbs and cheese together and sprinkle over the top. Bake in a 400°F oven for 15 - 20 minutes, until the top is golden brown.

FISH AU GRATIN

Make as for Cauliflower Cheese but substitute fish for the cauliflower.

LEEKS AU GRATIN

Make as for Cauliflower Cheese but substitute leeks, boiled for 5 minutes and sliced, for the cauliflower.

POTATO AND ONION AU GRATIN

Make as for Cauliflower Cheese but substitute thin slices of potato alternated with thin slices of onion for the cauliflower.

KENTISH ONION SALAD

1 large onion, cut in very thin rings
1/2 cup malt vinegar
black pepper

Liberally sprinkle the onion rings with black pepper, pour over the vinegar and let them sit for 1 - 2 hours. Drain off the vinegar and eat the onions with large slabs of oven-warmed bread and thick slices of cheddar cheese. Washed down with large mugs of Kentish ale.

that thin slices of potato alternated with thin slices of onion and baked in the sauce make a gorgeous dish, hot or cold. And best of all, you will come to appreciate the wonderful, homey smell that comes from baking cheese.

Another great smelling but sadly neglected simplicity is macaroni and cheese, which, although Kraft would like you to think otherwise, bears no resemblance at all to Kraft Dinner. Once a boardinghouse staple, a solid plank in Friday night suppers and, before that, a most luxurious French dish called *macaroni à la reine,* macaroni and cheese has almost disappeared from modern cookbooks, although it *is* reappearing on the menus of upmarket New York restaurants, in designer dishes at designer prices, along with such other homey one-pot dishes as shepherd's pie.

This recipe, from my grandmother's woodstove kitchen, takes about 35 minutes from start to finish if you start heating the oven when you put the macaroni on to cook. It looks best when cooked in an old Pyrex dish with the brown burned into it, or the beat-up old enamel casserole you are thinking of giving to Goodwill.

Cook eight ounces of elbow macaroni for 12 to 15 minutes in lots of salted, boiling water. Meanwhile, make the cheese sauce (the sauce Mornay) just as you did for the cauliflower and cheese, using milk instead of vegetable stock, cheddar cheese, nutmeg, a little cayenne pepper and as much cream as you won't feel guilty over. That recipe may give you more sauce than you need for macaroni, but the unused portion will keep in the fridge for four or five days, and by that time you will have used it on some fish or vegetables, or you will have grated a bit more cheese into it, spread it on toast and then broiled it for a quick snack — a sort of unauthentic Welsh rarebit.

To finish the macaroni and cheese, chop two or three tomatoes fairly finely (no need to skin them), grate some more cheese and find two or three tablespoons of breadcrumbs. Drain the macaroni and immediately fold it and the tomatoes into the sauce. Pour it into a buttered casserole, mix the cheese and breadcrumbs, spread them on top and bake at 400°F/200°C for 20 minutes or until the top is golden and slightly crusty.

If you need to be decorative, top with very thin tomato slices, *then* sprinkle with the cheese and breadcrumbs. Or take the dish out of the oven when it is crisp, lay on the tomato slices, dot them with butter and put the whole thing under the broiler for two or three minutes. That's basic, family-style macaroni and cheese. Tart it up with thinly sliced almonds for the last two minutes of broiling, pretty it up with sprigs of parsley or very thin slices of lemon, dust it with paprika for extra colour or add a little curry powder for something different. But none of this is really necessary — cooked cheese has its own simple, unavoidable virtue.

Rising To The Occasion

Nothing's more conducive to intimacy than a Sunday morning spent up to your elbows in flour, followed by the smell of baking bread.

Everybody should make bread at least once. Fancy cooks who regularly astound their friends should make it because it teaches humility, and sympathy for those who aren't quite as good. And self-admitted bad cooks, the "I always get it wrong" brigade? They, too, should make bread, because they will find that their muddling, their getting it wrong, is not as serious as they thought, and the loaves, peculiar though they may look, will bring a sense of pride for maybe the first time in their lives.

Kids should make bread, and old men should, too. It teaches them patience and the nature of time — and if they can learn it together, it shows them compassion for the inadequacies of the generation in between. Making bread is more fun than aerobics, a wonderful exercise for the lower back and the tummy muscles that those nubile young women are always, to that relentless music, insisting that we tuck in.

Bread-making is a slow process. Despite all the instant yeasts and timesavers, making bread takes half a day, and there's nothing you can do to hurry it along. The gimmicks and machines that promise instant bread try hard to move you into the fast lane, but all real things, like music and babies and religion and gardening, take time, and savouring that time works better than any tranquilizer for bringing inner peace.

People don't make bread for much the same reason as they don't draw or paint. They're scared; they think it won't be good enough, that there is a Federal Bread Board which sends out inspectors. They forget that their great-grandmothers, who had less education than most of today's grade three students and less equipment than most of us take for a weekend's camping, made wonderful bread on the tailgates of horsedrawn wagons.

If you didn't learn to make bread as a child, then it's time to start — and if you have children, it's time they started. This recipe, which I call poor man's pizza, is not exactly bread and not exactly pizza, but it is a very simple, pleasing thing to make.

In a bowl, mix one cup of flour, one teaspoon of baking powder, a half-teaspoon of salt, one tablespoon of vegetable oil and four to six

POOR MAN'S PIZZA

DOUGH

1 cup flour
1 tsp baking powder
1/2 tsp salt
1 tbsp vegetable oil
4 - 6 tbsp water
a handful of grated cheese
1/2 tsp oregano

TOPPING SUGGESTIONS

sliced tomatoes, fried bacon,
sliced mushrooms, canned
shrimp or salmon, avocado,
salami, etc.
a handful grated cheese

*In a bowl, mix the flour,
baking powder, salt, oil and
water and knead until you
get a stiffish dough. Add the
cheese and oregano and
knead for another minute,
then flatten with a rolling pin
until it's the thickness of your
little finger.*

*Heat the oil in a frypan, lay in
the dough and cook over
medium/low heat for 5
minutes. Turn it over, top with
whatever you want, sprinkle
on the cheese and cook
another 5 minutes. For a
softer bread cook with the lid
on, for a crisper, dryer bread
cook without the lid.*

BREAD

6 cups flour, unbleached or
all-purpose
2 tsp salt
3 tbsp sugar
1 pkt quick-rising yeast
3 tbsp vegetable oil
2 cups hot water

*Put 2 cups flour and all the
other dry ingredients
(including the yeast) into a
bowl or mixer and stir. Add
the hot water and stir
vigorously for 1 minute (or 1
minute at medium speed in a
mixer). Add the oil and mix,
then add another cup of
flour.*

tablespoons of water. It should be a stiffish dough, and the best way to mix it is with your hands, which brings us to lesson one in breadmaking: kneading, which you must do a lot. Kneading is mauling the dough about, squeezing it, flattening it out with the palm of your hand, folding it over and flattening it again, then squeezing it some more.

Now add a handful of grated cheese and a half-teaspoon of oregano. Knead for another minute, then flatten with a rolling pin, your hands or a bottle until it's about as thick as your little finger. If the dough sticks to the counter, scrape it off and sprinkle a little flour, then flatten it out again.

The first breadmakers didn't have ovens, so neither will we. Heat a tablespoon of oil in a frypan, put in the dough and cook over medium-low heat for five minutes. Now turn it over and top with whatever you like — sliced tomatoes, fried bacon, sliced mushrooms, canned shrimp or salmon, avocado, salami, ketchup — whatever. Then sprinkle it with more cheese and cook another five minutes. Some people put a lid on the pan to make the bread softer; others like it crisp and dryer. Whichever you choose is invariably the best, particularly if you are a seven-year-old making it for the first time.

All that kneading does two things. First, it makes gluten, the stuff that makes bread different from pastry or muffins. Second, it teaches you not to be scared, that dough likes rough treatment. A *real* loaf needs more gluten (which means more kneading), and yeast instead of baking powder.

Yeast comes in packets and tins. Buy packets — they're less formidable — and, for your first try, buy quick-rising yeast. Now get ready. You'll need six cups of unbleached or all-purpose flour, two teaspoons of salt (salt is essential to good bread), three tablespoons of sugar, one packet of quick-rising yeast, three tablespoons of vegetable oil and two cups of hot water (not boiling, just hot enough that you can dip your finger into it without burning yourself).

Put two cups of flour and all the other dry ingredients (including the yeast) into a bowl or mixer and stir together. Add the hot water and stir vigorously with a wooden spoon for one minute (one minute at medium speed in the mixer). Add the oil and mix for a few more strokes, then add another cup of flour. Beat for five minutes (three minutes in the mixer) and then start to add the rest of the flour, about a half-cup at a time.

Now, if you're using a mixer, you employ the dough hook. When the mixture becomes a dough (in the mixer, it wraps itself around the dough hook and looks almost shiny on the outside; by hand, it gets shaggy-looking), take it out of the bowl and start kneading it on the kitchen counter, which you have lightly dusted with flour.

Soft, regular pushing is the best way to knead, giving the dough a quarter-turn after each push and folding it back over itself. Kneading is a meditative process; there is no hurry and there are no prizes to win. It is a time to dream and think — and it is extremely good practice for timid backrubbers.

If the dough gets sticky, add a handful of flour. Occasionally — there are no rules, just do this when you feel like it — pick it up in one lump and hurl it, with both hands, down onto the counter. All of this creates the gluten, and the dough becomes shiny and stretchy.

Now put the dough back into the bowl, which has already been washed and lightly oiled by you or one of the marvelling crowd around you ("I never knew you could make bread!"). Roll it around in the bowl, then cover the bowl with plastic film or put it in a plastic bag. Leave it in a warm place and let it rise for 45 minutes.

Now we come to lesson two in breadmaking, which simply teaches you that for 45 minutes you have nothing to do and nobody can accuse you of doing nothing because you are *making bread*. Reading a book is good for bread-rising. So is a quiet snooze, playing with the cat, reading to the children or just daydreaming. Forty-five minutes isn't exactly how long the rising takes. It could be an hour or an hour and a half. When you look into the bowl, the dough should be shinier and at least twice as big as it originally was; it will look alive.

Now comes another pleasure. Make a fist and punch the dough down. You don't have to be kind. Turn it out onto the counter (which you have floured a little more) and knead it again for a minute. Cut it in half with a sharp knife and shape each piece into a ball, which you let sit for five minutes while you oil two bread pans and heat the oven to 400°F (200°C).

Pat each ball into an oval to fit its pan. Place the loaves in the pans, give each an affectionate little stroke and cover (again, in the plastic bag and a warm place) for 45 minutes. Then remove the plastic, put the loaves in the oven and bake for 10 minutes. Next, turn the oven down to 350°F (175°C) and cook for another 30 minutes.

Take one loaf out of the pan and tap the bottom with your middle finger. If it sounds hollow, it's done. If it isn't, put it back for five minutes.

Remove the loaves from their pans and let them cool on a wire rack. There is no taste quite like slightly warm bread with butter, a slab of cheese, butter and jam or peanut butter. But don't eat both loaves warm. Leave one on the counter, in a conspicuous place, so your friends and neighbours, your children and their friends, your spouse and your in-laws can't fail to see it. This is the moment when you join the ranks of the truly select — the breadmakers.

"I rather like to make my own bread," you say. And even though you don't feel modest, try not to look *too* superior.

Beat for 5 minutes (3 minutes in the mixer) and then add the rest of the flour, half a cup at a time.

If you're using a mixer, fit the dough hook and when the mixture has wrapped itself round the hook, take it out and knead it on a floured board. Knead slowly, adding extra flour if the dough becomes too sticky.

Put the dough back into the bowl, which has been washed and lightly oiled, roll it around and then cover with plastic film and leave in a warm place to rise for 45 minutes or up to 1 1/2 hours.

Turn out the risen dough and punch it down onto a floured board and knead. Cut in half and shape each into a ball. Oil two bread pans and heat the oven to 400°F.

Pat each ball into an oval to fit into the pans, cover again with plastic and place in a warm place for 45 minutes.

Remove the plastic, put the loaves in the oven and bake for 10 minutes. Turn down the oven to 350°F and cook for a further 30 minutes.

Check to see if the loaves are cooked by tapping the bottom. If they sound hollow, they're done. Remove from pans and let them cool on a wire rack.

Taking Stalk

Asparagus is known as the glamour vegetable, but it's just as charming dressed down.

STEAMED ASPARAGUS

1 bunch asparagus
salt
juice of half a lemon or orange

Break the asparagus stalks where they break easily, about one inch from the bottom. Stand them, points up, in an old coffee pot. Sprinkle a little salt over the tops, put two inches of water in the pot and cook the stalks, lid on, for 4 - 8 minutes. Pour off the water, remove the asparagus and serve with butter or a little olive oil and lemon or orange juice.

ASPARAGUS AND GINGER OR ASPARAGUS CHINESE- STYLE

1 bunch asparagus
5 - 6 thin slices ginger
2 tbsp oil
salt
water

Fry the ginger for 1 minute over medium/high heat in the oil. Lay in the asparagus stalks, no more than two deep, sprinkle them with salt and carefully turn them in the oil. Add 2 tbsp water, put the lid on and cook for 5 minutes.

ASPARAGUS KOREAN- STYLE

Cook as for Asparagus and Ginger and add a chopped garlic clove, a good pinch of red pepper flakes to the oil along with the ginger, and sprinkle with sesame oil afterwards.

Asparagus time is here — asparagus, the glamour vegetable that gets its picture in the social columns and appears on the plates of the rich and famous. Like most of the rich and famous, it's usually overdressed, in something rather complicated with a foreign name, because simple, unadorned virtue is never quite enough for North American tastes. Nobody buys the base model car, the three-speed bike or the camera without the gizmos; we have this awful need to complicate things.

Fresh asparagus is one of the world's great and simple luxuries. China, Japan, most of Europe, North and South America . . . they all grow asparagus, and they all associate it with springtime and the wonderful things that come at the beginning of a year, bringing with them those old-fashioned lovelies of words like "fecund" and "burgeoning" and "vernal." Even "pregnant" comes to have a different meaning in spring, as we watch the buds on the trees and the tips of what may well be weeds in a month grow with all the urgency and vitality of something brand new.

Those little bundles in the supermarket, skinny the first month, plump the next, green on the shafts and royally purple at the points, are our first and best vegetable, each spear a signpost to summer. We should learn to bypass the well-travelled route of hollandaise sauce and take some of the lesser-known roads to pleasure and contentment, like plain butter (not margarine or corn oil or anything other than pure, cholesterol-laden, lovely, yellow butter) melted over a plateful of steamed asparagus. Each person at the table should be fully supplied with asparagus and nothing else — no meat, no rice, no fancy *nouvelle cuisine* concoctions; just asparagus, slightly undercooked (for perhaps half the time most cookbooks recommend), still crisp, still slightly crunchy and brilliantly green. Keep a saltshaker handy, just in case, and a quarter of a juicy lemon for the occasional drop.

This is asparagus at its purest and simplest. You must, of course, choose it carefully. The cut bottoms of the stalks should still be moist. They should not be strangled by an over-enthusiastic elastic band, and each one should stand as straight and determined as a kid in a school choir. If the asparagus doesn't fill you with joy and admiration, don't buy it. There will be more tomorrow.

There are two ways to cook asparagus. For the first, you'll need a coffee pot, a garage sale special. Break the stalks where they break easily, about an inch from the bottom, and stand them points up in the coffee pot. Sprinkle a little salt over the tops, put two inches of water in the bottom of the pot and cook the stalks, lid on, for four to eight minutes, depending on their size. Pour off the water, take off the lid and you have perfectly cooked asparagus, the tops steamed and the bottoms boiled, ready to melt the butter and be eaten immediately.

If you don't want butter, try olive oil. Cook the asparagus in the coffee pot, put it on a plate, salt it a little, pepper it, drizzle it with olive oil and squeeze half a lemon over it. That's what the Italians do, with the best and most flavourful olive oil they have, and down south where oranges grow — nice, red-streaked, juicy oranges — they use orange juice instead of lemon juice. So can you.

If you don't have a coffee pot, or if you want something different, a frypan will do. Any store that sells asparagus will also sell fresh ginger. Fry five or six thin slices of ginger for a minute over medium-high heat in two tablespoons of oil — olive oil, peanut oil, safflower oil . . . they're all good. Now lay the asparagus stalks in the pan, snugged up close, no more than two deep. Sprinkle them with salt and carefully turn them in the hot oil so each stalk is coated. Add two tablespoons of water, put the lid on and cook them for five minutes. This is basic Chinese asparagus. To make it Japanese, sprinkle the cooked asparagus with a few drops of sesame oil and a little lemon juice, or a teaspoon of sesame seeds. To make it Korean, add a chopped garlic clove and a pinch of red pepper to the oil along with the ginger and sprinkle with sesame oil afterwards.

If you feel that you have to make a sauce, there are quicker and easier types than hollandaise. In Germany they beat a teaspoon of horseradish, the juice of a quarter of a lemon, a teaspoon of sugar and a half-teaspoon of salt into a cup of lightly whipped cream. In southern France they whip the cream until it's thick, with half a teaspoon of curry powder, a little lemon juice and either tarragon or tarragon vinegar, then serve it with cold asparagus. In northern Italy they melt a few tablespoons of butter while the asparagus cooks, add four or five finely chopped cloves of garlic, cook them for just one minute and turn off the heat. The instant the asparagus goes onto the plate, they add two tablespoons of finely chopped parsley, a pinch of salt and four or five pinches of ground pepper to the butter. This sauce also goes well with fresh green beans that have been dropped into boiling water for five minutes and immediately cooled under the cold tap, and with hot broccoli.

ASPARAGUS GERMAN-STYLE

1 tsp horseradish
juice of a quarter of a lemon
1 tsp sugar
1/2 tsp salt
1 cup cream, lightly whipped

Cook the asparagus as for Steamed Asparagus and beat the above ingredients into a sauce and serve with the asparagus.

ASPARAGUS FRENCH-STYLE

1 cup cream, thickly whipped
1/2 tsp curry powder
a little lemon juice
tarragon or tarragon vinegar

Cook the asparagus as for Steamed Asparagus and beat the above ingredients into a sauce. Serve with cold asparagus.

ASPARAGUS ITALIAN-STYLE

4 - 5 cloves garlic, finely chopped
2 - 3 tbsp butter
2 tbsp parsley, finely chopped
a pinch of salt
4 - 5 pinches of pepper

Cook the asparagus as for Steamed Asparagus. Melt the butter, add the garlic and cook for 1 minute. Turn off the heat. Put the asparagus on a plate and immediately add the parsley, salt and pepper to the sauce and pour over the asparagus.

ASPARAGUS WITH EGGS

2 eggs
butter
1 tsp lemon juice
1/2 tsp wine vinegar
1 tbsp capers
pepper
parmesan cheese

Cook the asparagus as for Steamed Asparagus. Melt some butter and cook the eggs sunny-side up. Arrange the asparagus on a plate with the eggs on top. Add more butter to the pan and stir in the lemon juice, wine vinegar and capers. Stir for 1 minute and pour over the eggs. Sprinkle with pepper and a little parmesan cheese.

ASPARAGUS JAPANESE-STYLE

Cook as for Asparagus and Ginger and sprinkle with a few drops of sesame oil and a little lemon juice, or 1 tsp sesame seeds.

ASPARAGUS WITH MUSHROOMS

2 eggs, hard-boiled
1/2 lb fresh mushrooms, thinly sliced
2 tbsp butter
3 tbsp parsley, finely chopped
1 small onion, finely chopped
1 cup whipping cream
a pinch of grated nutmeg
1 egg yolk
a little salt and pepper

Cook the asparagus as for Steamed Asparagus. Meanwhile heat the butter over medium heat, add the onion and cook for 2 minutes. Add the parsley and mushrooms and cook for a further 2 minutes, stirring gently.

Add the cream, nutmeg and egg yolk to the mushrooms and stir vigorously for 3 - 4 minutes until the sauce thickens. Remove from the heat and add the salt, pepper and lemon juice.

Serve the sauce over the butt ends of the asparagus with the spears surrounded by quarters of hard-boiled egg.

These dishes are all easy, but if you want to put in 20 minutes of real cooking and impress somebody, few things are prettier than asparagus with mushrooms. You will need two hard-boiled eggs, half a pound of thinly sliced, fresh mushrooms, two tablespoons of butter, three tablespoons of finely chopped parsley, a small, finely chopped onion, a cup of whipping cream, a pinch of nutmeg, an egg yolk and a little salt.

Heat the butter over medium heat, add the onions and cook for two minutes. Add the parsley and mushrooms and cook for another two minutes, stirring gently. Now put the asparagus into the coffee pot and get it started. Add the cream, nutmeg and egg yolk to the mushrooms and stir vigorously for three or four minutes, until the sauce thickens. Take it off the heat, add the salt and pepper and stir in a little lemon juice. As soon as the asparagus is cooked, serve it with the sauce over the butt ends, the spears surrounded by quarters of hard-boiled egg. Very rich, very smooth, very comforting.

And finally, if you are a determined bachelor equipped with nothing but a frypan, I remember an appetizer from Naples that can easily become a main course. While the asparagus is in the coffee pot, melt a good tablespoon of butter in a frypan and cook two eggs sunny-side up. Arrange the asparagus on a plate and the eggs on the asparagus. Add a bit more butter to the frypan, stir in a teaspoon of lemon juice, a half teaspoon of wine vinegar and a tablespoon of capers, stir for a minute and pour it over the eggs. Sprinkle with pepper and a little parmesan cheese. It's much quicker than a pizza.